enny Kee's designs are based on two intertwined themes — the Australian national identity and the environment. Kee opened her *Flamingo Park* salon in Sydney's Strand Arcade in1973 and was soon receiving international acclaim for her Australiana theme knitwear and fabric designs. She moved to the Blue Mountains in 1976 and her designs began to reflect her keen belief in conservation. In 1980, world-renowned Italian fabric printer, Fabio Bellotti, began printing Kee designs on silk and in 1983 Karl Lagerfeld used her *Opal Oz* fabric at the first Chanel ready-to-wear collection. Since then Kee has been commissioned to design tapestries, rugs and fabrics, which include a rug for the new Parliament House in Canberra and the official Australian Bicentennial scarf. Her clothes have been exhibited at the Art Gallery of New South Wales and the Australian National Gallery in 1988, and in 1989 at the Victoria and Albert Museum in London.

JENNY KEE
Photography by Richard Bailey
Books from Down Under
Prentice Hall Press
New York London Toronto Sydney Tokyo Singapore
KNITS FROM NATURE

The first number refers to the photograph.
The second number refers to the pattern.

INTRODUCTION 7

BASIC INFORMATION 46

KOOMPARTOO VEST 10, 48 JACKET 10, 50

DOVES AND DOLPHINS JUMPER 12, 53

APHRODITE JUMPER 14, 56

ULTIMATE OZ JUMPER 16, 58

WARATAH AND BLACKBOY JUMPER 18, 60

FLORAL OZ JUMPER 19, 62

PAX VEST 20, 68 SOCKS 20, 68 SCARF 20, 69

PAX JOY CARDIGAN 21, 64 PONCHO 21, 67 JUMPER 22, 66
SKIRT 22, 66 LEG-INS 21, 67

I LOVE DOLPHINS JUMPER 24, 74

CONTENTS

BANKSIA JUMPER 26, 77

BARRAMUNDI JUMPER 27, 71

DIDGERIDOO DOLMAN 28, 80

GUMLEAF JUMPER 30, 82

FOOTBALL FISH TABARD 32, 84

BARRIER REEF TOP 34, 87 SKIRT 34, 87 JUMPER 35, 86

DOLPHINS TABARD 36, 89 TOP 38, 92

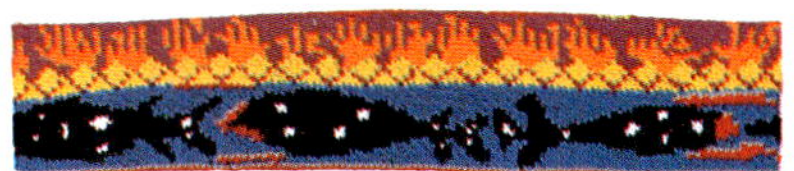

STINGRAY TOP 39, 94

UNDER THE SEA DRESS 40, 99

SPOTTY FISH CARDIGAN 41, 96

TROPICAL SEA GARDEN DRESS 42, 102

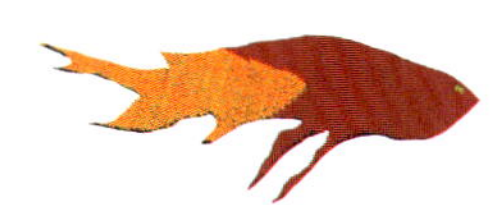

ACKNOWLEDGEMENTS 104

INDEX 104

In the hope of a growing awareness of nature by all people, this book is dedicated to all those who work tirelessly to save our environment.

Prentice Hall Press
15 Columbus Circle
New York, New York 10023

First published in Australia in 1990 by
Simon & Schuster Australia
7 Grosvenor Place, Brookvale NSW 2100

Prentice Hall Press and colophons are registered trademarks of Simon & Schuster, Inc.

A Paramount Communications Company
Sydney New York London Toronto Tokyo Singapore

Library of Congress
Card Catalog Number: 90-70746
ISBN: 0-13-517228-4

Designed by Susie Agoston-O'Connor
Finished art by Chris Hatcher/Graphix
Graphs by Katherine Jarvis and Sue Morton
Typeset in Australia by Savage Type Pty Ltd, Brisbane
Produced by Mandarin Offset in Hong Kong

First Prentice Hall Press Edition

INTRODUCTION

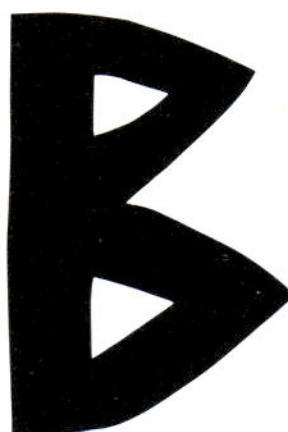

eing in nature — feeling part of the web of life — gives me my inspiration and joy for living. Nature has given me my subjects to design, from the earth to the ocean.

I have a deep respect and sense of wonder for the natural world. When I walk through the bush and the forests and swim in the ocean and the rivers, I feel connected and at peace. I feel whole and I find the language to express my ideas.

Whenever I see the environment being destroyed, the stronger I become in my passion for wanting to preserve it. I am a conservationist. I cannot paint dolphins and gum trees without wanting to save them. Nature gives me everything and I want to give something back. We all have a moral duty in this next decade to fight for the preservation of the last of this planet's wilderness areas, to stop polluting our oceans and to ensure peace for humankind.

In this book I have chosen simple classic shapes to complement my designs from nature. I have added my symbols for peace, love and harmony, messages from my heart to bring joy to all who knit.

Living and loving nature, and being in harmony with it, is the only truth I know. I believe in the words of the American Indian Chief Seattle who wrote in 1854, 'This we know — the earth does not belong to man — man belongs to the earth. All things are connected — whatever befalls the earth befalls the sons of the earth.'

I hope that through my designs you will be inspired to preserve our natural environment too.

Peace and love

Jenny Kee

KOOMPARTOO

KOOMPARTOO
11

DOVES AND DOLPHINS

DOVES AND DOLPHINS

APHRODITE

WARATAH AND BLACKBOY

FLORAL OZ

PAX

PAX JOY

P A X   J O Y

I LOVE DOLPHINS

BANKSIA

B A R R A M U N D I

DIDGERIDOO

FOOTBALL FISH

FOOTBALL FISH

BARRIER REEF

BARRIER REEF

DOLPHINS

STINGRAY

S P O T T Y F I S H

YARNS
The yarns used in this book have been selected for their high quality and wide colour range. However, any yarn can be used as long as it knits up to the same tension stated in the pattern. If desired, knitting elastic may be worked in with yarn for firmness in ribbed bands.

TENSION/GAUGE
The tension/gauge specifies the number of stitches and rows in the pattern using the stated yarn and each garment has been checked to ensure the correct tension/gauge for the knitting technique used in the pattern. To ensure the success of your finished garment, it is important that the correct tension/gauge is obtained before starting work. Otherwise, the garment could be too large or too small. To make a tension/gauge test, knit a square slightly larger than the one stated in the tension/gauge notes, using the needles and wool ply given. Knit the square, reproducing the main pattern with all stated colour changes, as this will affect the finished tension/gauge.
Lay the square out flat without stretching, and measure out a 10 x 10 cm (4 x 4 in) square, then count the number of stitches and rows between the pins. Measure the square out several times to make sure the reading is accurate.
If there are too many stitches to the centimetre or inch, the tension/gauge is too tight and needles a size larger should be used. If there are too few stitches, the tension/gauge is too loose and needles a size smaller should be used. If the number of rows does not correspond to the stated length check the length during knitting.

GRAPHS
To knit from the charts, read from the right hand corner to the left for a knit row and from left to right for a purl row, unless otherwise stated. Left handed knitters should reverse these instructions.
Each square on the chart represents a stitch and each line corresponds to a row of knitting. Colour changes are indicated with a code.
If working with a number of colours, colour the chart in with the shades you plan to use, as this will make the colour work easier to follow.
Because of the complicated nature of some of the graphs it may be advisable to work from enlarged photocopies.

STRANDING THE YARN
All garments in this book feature many different coloured yarns and use either fair isle or 'picture knitting' techniques. Using the correct finishing method is an integral part of producing a neat, well-made garment and, unless you are working on an isolated area of colour, it is not advisable to join yarn in the middle of a row as it can distort the stitches. Allow enough yarn to complete the row and join a new ball at the side edge. Either knit in the old ball as you go or leave sufficient yarn to darn into the back of the garment.

MEASUREMENTS
The patterns in this book are all one size and loose-fitting. Some are designed to be worked in several yarns or techniques, so you should not be too concerned if one area of your garment differs *slightly* in tension from another.

INTARSIA OR COLOUR CROSSING
This is the method of working with a number of colours with a separate ball for each area. When crossing from one yarn to the next on the pattern, the old and new yarns must be crossed over at the join to prevent a hole forming. If a number of colours are required over a small area, wind the yarn into smaller, more manageable size balls and secure loosely with a rubber band to prevent them unravelling.

STRANDING
Stranding is when several yarns are used to create a pattern (such as in fair isle knitting) and the yarn is carried across the back of the garment when not in use. It is important to maintain the correct tension when using this method, as the garment will pucker if the yarn is pulled too tight. Check often by flattening out the garment to see if there are any tight spots.

When stranding the yarn on a knit row, knit the stated number of stitches in the main colour, then drop the yarn to the back of the work. Knit the next part of the pattern in a contrast yarn, then pick up the first colour, allowing enough yarn for it to sit loosely at the back of the garment. Do not take up the slack as this will cause the garment to pucker when it is flattened out.

WEAVING IN

Weaving the yarn into the knitting is the best method for 'picture knitting' or when there are frequent repeats of five or more stitches. This method avoids having long 'floats' of yarn across the back of the work, which can catch and cause holes or distortions.

Weaving in creates a well finished garment but keep in mind, that the more colours carried across the thicker and bulkier the woollen. If there are only small patches of colour required in the pattern, it may be more advisable to use the **Intarsia** method already given.

Loose, rather than tight weaving is advisable as the tension/gauge can be affected and the work will look puckered. To weave in on a knit row, hold the main colour normally and the contrast yarn with the forefinger of your other hand. Knit one stitch as you work then knit the next stitch over the contrast. The same method is used on a purl row but the yarn is held in front of the work. Feed the contrast over the main yarn and work one stitch, then purl the next stitch keeping the contrast below the main yarn.

GARMENT CARE

Wool and cotton deserve special care because they are special fabrics. These helpful hints are designed to make the washing of woollens and cottons hassle-free.

- There are a number of washing liquids and powders specially developed for washing wool and which are widely available. Always use one of these for washing your garment.
- Don't wash your woollens in hot water, as the colours will run. Only wash them in cold or warm water and never soak them for more than five minutes.
- Remember to check that the powder or liquid is fully dissolved before you put the garment in the water.
- Avoid letting the tap run directly on to your woollens as it can matt the fibres.
- Always rinse at the end of the wash. The powder or liquid detergent will lift the dirt from the fibres and retain the natural spring to the wool.
- Place the garment into a pillowslip or towel and spin in the washing machine for a couple of minutes to remove excess water, then lay the garment flat on a dry towel. Wool is a delicate fibre when wet, so never twist or wring a garment as this can misshape it.

- Never dry wool in direct sunlight because colours will fade and whites may 'yellow'. Likewise if you get caught in a shower, dry your garments away from direct heat — never place them in front of a fire or radiator, as the fibres will become brittle.
- Cotton garments should be washed in hot water, as cold water sometimes causes dyed cotton to 'bleed'. Like wool, cotton should be rinsed well and laid flat away from direct sunlight to dry. When pressing the garment use a hot iron.

ABBREVIATIONS

K	knit
P	purl
st st	stocking stitch (one row knit, one row purl)
beg	beginning
cont	continue/ing
foll	follow/ing
inc	increase
dec	decrease
tog	together
rep	repeat
rem	remaining
alt	alternate
patt	pattern
RS row	right side row
WS row	wrong side row
sl st	slip stich
psso	pass slip stitch over
yon	yarn over needle
yrn	yarn round needle
lp	loop

Knitting Needle Sizes

English	000	00	0	1	2	3	4	5	6	7	8	9	10	11	12	13	14
Metric	10	9	8	7.5	7	6.5	6	5.5	5	4.5	4	3.75	3.25	3	2.75	2.25	2
American	15	13	12	11	10.5	10	9	8	7	6	5	4	3	2	1	1	00

KOOMPARTOO VEST

MATERIALS
2 colours, see key.
50 g (2 oz) balls of Villawool 8 ply Superwash, or equivalent yarn to give stated tension: A 8 balls; B 6 balls.
Pair each 4.50 mm (No. 7), 3.75 mm (No. 9) and 3.25 mm (No. 10) knitting needles. 6 buttons. Two safety pins.

MEASUREMENTS (Garment Measures)
Bust: 131 cm (51½ in)
Length: 59 cm (23¼ in)

TENSION/GAUGE
22 sts and 28 rows to 10 cm (4 in) over st st in fair isle patt, using 4.50 mm (No. 7) needles. Change needle size if necessary to obtain the stated tension/gauge.

NOTES
Always use 4.50 mm (No. 7) needles for fair isle patt and 3.75 mm (No. 9) needles for all other st st sections.
Use separate balls for different sections when working large motifs.

BACK
With 3.25 mm (No. 10) needles and A, cast on 145 sts. Work in K1, P1 rib for 20 rows. Change to 3.75 mm (No. 9) needles and st st. Changing to 4.50 mm (No. 7) needles for fair isle sections, work 152 rows of graph 1. Cast/bind off loosely.

LEFT FRONT
With 3.25 mm (No. 10) needles, cast on 6 sts in B, then 77 sts in A.
1st row: K1, (P1, K1) 38 times in A, (P1, K1) 3 times in B.
2nd row: (P1, K1) 3 times in B, with A P1, (K1, P1) 38 times.
Rep these 2 rows 8 times more, then 1st row only once more.
20th row: (P1, K1) 3 times in B, (P1, K1) 3 times in A, then leave these 12 sts on safety pin for front band, inc 1 st in next st, then cont in rib as before to end.
Change to 3.75 mm (No. 9) needles and st st, and changing to 4.50 mm (No. 7) needles for fair isle sections, cont to work on these 72 sts from graph 2 until 78th row has been worked.

SHAPE NECK
Working from graph 2 as before, dec 1 st at neck edge on next and every foll alt row 11 times in all, then on every foll 4th row 9 times. Cont on these rem 52 sts as on graph until 152 rows have been worked. Cast/bind off loosely.

The earth must be our first priority. We must revere and take care of the last tracks of wilderness in Australia and throughout the world.

RIGHT FRONT
With 3.25 mm (No. 10) needles, cast on 77 sts in A, 6 sts in B.
1st row: (K1, P1) 3 times in B, with A K1, (P1, K1) 38 times.
2nd row: With A P1, (K1, P1) 38 times, (K1, P1) 3 times in B.
Rep last 2 rows once more, then 1st row once (5 rows).

VERTICAL BUTTONHOLE
6th row: P1, (K1, P1) 38 times in A, *turn*, do not work over B. Work 4 more rows in rib over these 77 sts, then drop A, pick up B without twisting yarns and work 5 rows in rib over B only, ending on WS row.
11th row: (K1, P1) 3 times in B, pick up A and twist yarns as before, then work in rib 77 sts in A, (complete buttonhole).
Cont in rib and colours as before for further 8 rows ending with RS row.
20th row: Rib 70 sts in A, then in A inc 1 st in next st, leave rem 12 sts on safety pin for front band.
Change to 3.75 mm (No. 9) needles, st st, and using 4.50 mm (No. 7) needles for fair isle sections cont on these 72 sts from graph 3 until 78th row has been worked.

SHAPE NECK
Working from graph 3 as before, dec 1 st at neck edge on next row, then on every foll alt row 11 times in all, then on every foll 4th row 9 times. Cont on rem 52 sts as on graph 3 until 152 rows have been worked. Cast/bind off loosely.

TO MAKE UP
Sew in all ends. Press lightly on wrong sides. Sew shoulder seams. Place marker at each side edge on back and front pieces at 27 cm (10½ in) below shoulder seams.

ARMHOLE BANDS
With 3.25 mm (No. 10) needles and A, evenly pick up and knit 145 sts between markers. Work in K1, P1 rib for 3 cm (1¼ in). Cast/bind off in rib.

LEFT FRONT BAND
With 3.25 mm (No. 10) needles, rejoin A at inner edge, inc 1 st in first st, rib 5 sts, change to B and twist yarns as before, rib 6 sts (13 sts). Changing colours as before, work 93 rows more, ending with WS row. Place marker at end of last row for the beg of neck section. Cont as before until piece above marker fits along neck edge and to the centre of back neck. Cast/bind off in rib.

RIGHT FRONT BAND
With 3.25 mm (No. 10) needles, with WS facing, rejoin A at inner edge, inc 1 st in first st, rib 5 sts, change to B and twist yarns as before, rib 6 sts (13 sts). Work 5 rows in rib.

VERTICAL BUTTONHOLE
***Next row:** Work in rib to end of one colour, *turn*, do not work over other colour.
Work 4 more rows in rib on same colour, ending at centre of band, drop yarn, pick up other colour without twisting yarns, then work 5 rows in rib, ending at side edge of band.
Next row: Work in rib to end of the colour, drop yarn, pick up other colour and twist yarns, then work in rib to end. The buttonhole is completed *. Changing colours as before work 14 rows more in rib **. Rep from * to ** 3 times more, then rep from * to * once, (6 buttonholes). Work 2 rows more. Place marker at beg of last row. Cont in rib in colours until piece above marker fits along neck edge and to the centre of back neck. Cast/bind off in rib.

TO FINISH
Join front bands tog, place this seam to centre of back neck then place marker on front bands at the beg of neck shaping on fronts. Sew bands in position. Matching patts, sew up side seams and armhole bands. Sew on buttons.

KEY
☐ **A (Black)**
⊡ **B (White)**

right front
vest
left front
EARTH
FIRST
KOOMP
ARTOO
151
141
131
121
111
101
91
81
71
61
51
41
31
21
11
1
graph 3
graph 2
back
WILDERNESS
-KOOMPARTOO-
graph 1

KOOMPARTOO

Koompartoo means 'a new beginning'. We must have a new beginning to earth awareness — *Earth First*. The Taoist Yin-Yang symbolises the balance of man and nature and the symbol of peace stands for an anti-nuclear world.

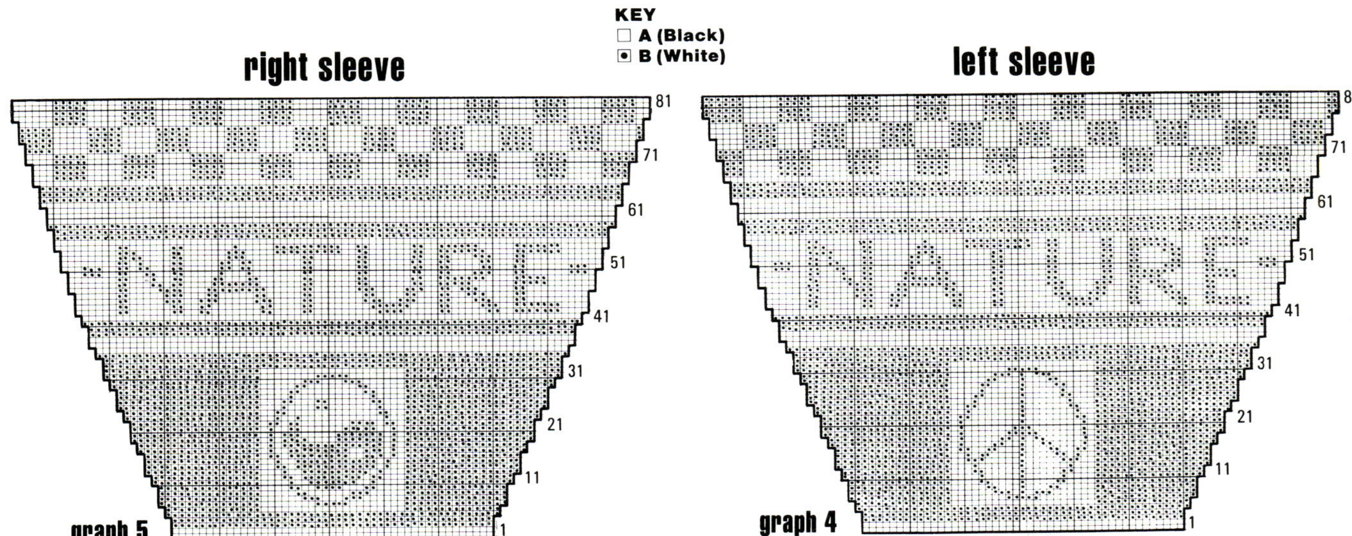

KOOMPARTOO JACKET

MATERIALS
2 colours, see key.
50 g (2 oz) balls of Paton's Pure Wool Jet, or equivalent yarn to give stated tension: A 15 balls; B 11 balls.
Pair each 6.00 mm (No. 4), 5.50 mm (No. 5) and 5.00 mm (No. 6) knitting needles.
55 cm (22 in) long open-end zipper.

MEASUREMENTS (Garment Measures)
Bust: 130 cm (51 in)
Length: 79 cm (31 in)
Sleeve seam: 50 cm (19½ in)

TENSION/GAUGE
18 sts and 20 rows to 10 cm (4 in) over st st in fair isle patt, using 6.00 mm (No. 4) needles. Change needle size if necessary to obtain the stated tension/gauge.

NOTES
Always use 6.00 mm (No. 4) needles for fair isle patt and 5.50 mm (No. 5) needles for all other st st sections.
Use separate balls of wool for different sections when working large motifs.

SPECIAL ABBREVIATION
yfon = take yarn in front and over the right needle.

BACK
With 5.00 mm (No. 6) needles and A, cast on 115 sts. Work in K1, P1 rib for 7.5 cm (3 in) ending with WS row. Change to 5.50 mm (No. 5) needles and st st. Work 134 rows from graph 1.

SHAPE NECK
Next row: Work 45 sts from graph 1, work 2 sts tog, cast/bind off next 21 sts, sl1, K1, psso, work from graph to end.
Cont on last 46 sts from graph for left side of neck, dec 1 st at neck edge on next 4 rows (42 sts rem). Work 1 row. Cast/bind off loosely.
Ret to rem 46 sts, rejoin yarn at neck edge. Work from graph for right side of neck and dec 1 st at neck edge on next 4 rows. Work 1 row. Cast/bind off loosely.

POCKET LININGS
Make 2. With 5.50 mm (No. 5) needles and A, cast on 24 sts. Work in st st. Work 3 rows each in A and B, then 17 rows in A, 3 rows in B and 2 rows in A. There are 28 rows. Leave sts on spare needle.

LEFT FRONT
With 5.00 mm (No. 6) needles, cast on 2 sts in B, 56 sts in A.
1st row: (K1, P1) 27 times A, K2 A, K2 B.
2nd row: K2 B, K2 A, (K1, P1) 27 times A.
Rep last 2 rows until 7.5 cm (3 in) ending with WS row. Change to 5.50 mm (No. 5) needles and cont as follows:
1st, 3rd rows: K56 A, K2 B.
2nd row: K2 B, K2 A, P54 A.
4th, 6th rows: K2 B, K2 A, P54 B.
5th row: K54 B, K2 A, K2 B.
Cont to work 4 sts in garter st at front edge in colours as set for zipper trim and all other sts in st st. Beg with 7th row cont to work from graph 2 until 28th row has been worked.

MAKE POCKET OPENING
Next row: With A K15, place pocket lining at back of work and knit next st of left front tog with first st of lining, slip next 22 sts on st holder for trim, K22 over lining, knit next st tog with last st of lining, K17 A, K2 B.
Next row: K2 B, K2 A, P54 B.
Beg with 31st row cont to work from graph 2 until 104 rows have been worked.

SHAPE NECK
Dec 1 st at neck edge on every row 11 times, then on every foll alt row 5 times. Cont straight on rem 42 sts as on graph until 140 rows have been worked. Cast/bind off loosely.
Ret to 22 sts for trim, with RS facing, 5.00 mm (No. 6) needles, rejoin A, knit 2 rows, then knit 4 rows in B. Cast/bind off. Attach ends of trim and lining in place.

RIGHT FRONT
With 5.00 mm (No. 6) needles, cast on 56 sts A, 2 sts B.
1st row: K2 B, K2 A, A (P1, K1) 27 times.
2nd row: A (P1, K1) 27 times, K2 A, K2 B.
Rep last 2 rows until 7.5 cm (3 in) ending with WS row. Change to 5.50 mm (No. 5) needles and cont as follows:
1st, 3rd rows: K2 B, K56 A.
2nd row: P54 A, K2 A, K2 B.
4th, 6th rows: P54 B, K2 A, K2 B.
Beg with 7th row cont to work from graph 3 with 4 sts in garter st at front edge for zipper trim as set and work until 28th row has been worked.

MAKE POCKET OPENING
Next row: K2 B, K17 A, with A knit next st of right front tog with first st of lining, slip next 22 sts on st holder for trim, K22 from lining, knit next st tog with last st of lining, K15 A.
Next row: P54 B, K2 A, K2 B.
Beg with 31st row cont to work from graph 3 until 104th row has been worked, then shape neck and finish off as for left front.

LEFT SLEEVE
With 5.00 mm (No. 6) needles and A, cast on 39 sts. Work in K1, P1 rib for 7.5 cm (3 in) ending with RS row.
Inc row: Rib 5, (inc 1 st in next st, rib 3) 8 times, rib 2 (47 sts). Change to 5.50 mm (No. 5) needles and st st. Working from graph 4 inc 1 st each end of 5th row, then ** inc 1 st each end of foll 2nd row once, then inc 1 st each end of foll 4th row once, rep from ** 6 times more. There should be 77 sts and 47 rows of st st at this stage. Cont to inc 1 st each end of every foll 4th row until there are 93 sts. Cont on these 93 sts straight from graph until 82 rows have been worked. Cast/bind off loosely.

RIGHT SLEEVE
Work as for left sleeve but reading from graph 5.

TO MAKE UP
Sew in all ends. Press lightly on wrong sides. Sew shoulders. Place centre of sleeve to shoulder seam and match patterns, then sew sleeves evenly in place.

LEFT COLLAR
With 5.00 mm (No. 6) needles, cast on 2 sts in A, 2 sts in B, 2 sts in A.
1st row: K2 A, K2 B, K2 A.
2nd row: With A inc 1 st in each of 2 A, K2 B, K2 A.
3rd row: K2 A, K2 B, with A K2, yon, K1, yon, K1.
4th row: With A K1, (drop extra lp, K1 in front and back lp of next st) twice, K1 A, K2 B, K2 A.
5th row: K2 A, K2 B, with A K2, yon, knit to last st, yon, K1 A.
6th row: With A K1, * drop extra lp, K1 in front and back lp of next st *, knit to next extra lp, rep from * to * once, K2 B, K2 A.
There should be 12 sts at this stage. Change to 5.50 mm (No. 5) needles. Rep 5th and 6th rows until there are 46 sts in all, then cont on these 46 sts straight in colours as before until edge fits without stretching along neck edge and to centre of back neck, then cont further 3 cm (1¼ in) for fullness. Loosely cast/bind off.

RIGHT COLLAR
With 5.00 mm (No. 6) needles, cast on 2 sts in A, 2 sts in B, 2 sts in A.
1st row: K2 A, K2 B, K2 A.
2nd row: K2 A, K2 B, with A inc 1 st in each of 2 A.
3rd row: With A K2, yon, K1, yon, K1, K2 B, K2 A.
4th row: K2 A, K2 B, with A K1, (drop extra lp, K1 in front and back lp of next st) twice, K1 A.
5th row: With A K2, yon, knit to last st before B, yon, K1 A, K2 B, K2 A.
6th row: K2 A, K2 B, with A K1, * drop extra lp, K1 in front and back lp of next st *, knit to next extra lp, rep from * to * once, K1 A.
Change to 5.50 mm (No. 5) needles and rep 5th and 6th rows until there are 46 sts in all, then cont on these 46 sts straight in colours as before until edge fits without stretching along neck edge and to centre of back neck, then cont further 3 cm (1¼ in) for fullness. Cast/bind off loosely.

TO FINISH
Matching colours, join wide ends of collar pieces tog with flat seam. Place seam of collar to centre of back neck and points of collar to the beg of neck shapings, neatly sew collar around neck edge, gathering fullness evenly along shoulder seams. Fold collar in half to inside and stitch down. Sew zipper along front edges. Matching patterns, sew up side and sleeve seams.

right front
jacket
left front
140
131
121
111
101
91
81
71
61
51
41
31
21
11
1
EARTH
KOOMP
FIRST
ARTOO
graph 3
graph 2
back
WILDERNESS
KOOMPARTOO
graph 1

From the sea to the sky, doves, dolphins and hearts dancing together symbolise peace, harmony and love in nature.

MATERIALS
10 colours, see key.
50 g (2 oz) balls of Robin Dynasty 12 ply Mohair, or equivalent yarn to give stated tension: A 3 balls; B 2 balls; C 2 balls; D 2 balls; E 2 balls; F 1 ball; G 1 ball; H 1 ball; I 2 balls; J 1 ball.
Pair each 5.50 mm (No. 5) and 4.50 mm (No. 7) knitting needles. Set of four 4.50 mm (No. 7) knitting needles.

MEASUREMENTS (Garment Measures)
Bust: 122 cm (48 in)
Length: 76 cm (30 in)
Sleeve seams: 51 cm (20 in)

TENSION/GAUGE
15 sts and 19 rows to 10 cm (4 in) over st st in picture knit, using 5.50 mm (No. 5) needles. Change needle size if necessary to obtain the stated tension/gauge.

BACK
With 4.50 mm (No. 7) needles and A, cast on 103 sts. Work in K1, P1 rib for 5 cm (2 in), ending with RS row.
Dec row: Rib 13 sts, (work 2 sts tog, rib 13 sts) 6 times (97 sts rem). Change to 5.50 mm (No. 5) needles and st st *. Work from graph 1 for 134 rows. Cast/bind off loosely.

FRONT
Work as for back to *. Work from graph 2 until 118 rows have been worked.

SHAPE NECK
Next row: Work 42 sts from graph, cast/bind off centre 13 sts loosely, work from graph to end.
Cont on last 42 sts from graph for right side of neck and cast/bind off at neck edge on every alt row 2 sts 3 times, 1 st 3 times (33 sts rem). Work 3 rows straight from graph. Cast/bind off loosely.
Ret to rem 42 sts, rejoin yarn at left neck edge. Work from graph for left side of neck and cast/bind off at beg of next and every foll alt row 2 sts 3 times, 1 st 3 times. Work 4 rows straight from graph. Cast/bind off loosely.

SLEEVES
Both the same.
With 4.50 mm (No. 7) needles and A, cast on 34 sts. Work in K1, P1 rib for 10 cm (4 in), ending with RS row.
Inc row: Rib 3 sts, (inc 1 st in next st, rib 2 sts) 10 times, rib 1 st (44 sts).
Change to 5.50 mm (No. 5) needles and st st. Work from graph 3 *at same time* inc 1 st each end of 3rd row once, then on every foll 4th row until there are 82 sts. Work 5 rows straight from graph. Cast/bind off loosely.

TO MAKE UP
Sew in all ends. Sew shoulder seams.

NECKBAND
With set of four 4.50 mm (No. 7) needles and A, evenly pick up and knit 47 sts on front neck, 37 sts on back neck (84 sts). Work in rnds of K1, P1 rib for 15 cm (6 in). Cast/bind off ribwise loosely.

TO FINISH
Match centre of sleeve top to shoulder seam and sew sleeves evenly in place, then sew up side and sleeve seams. Fold neckband in half to inside and sew loosely in place.

back

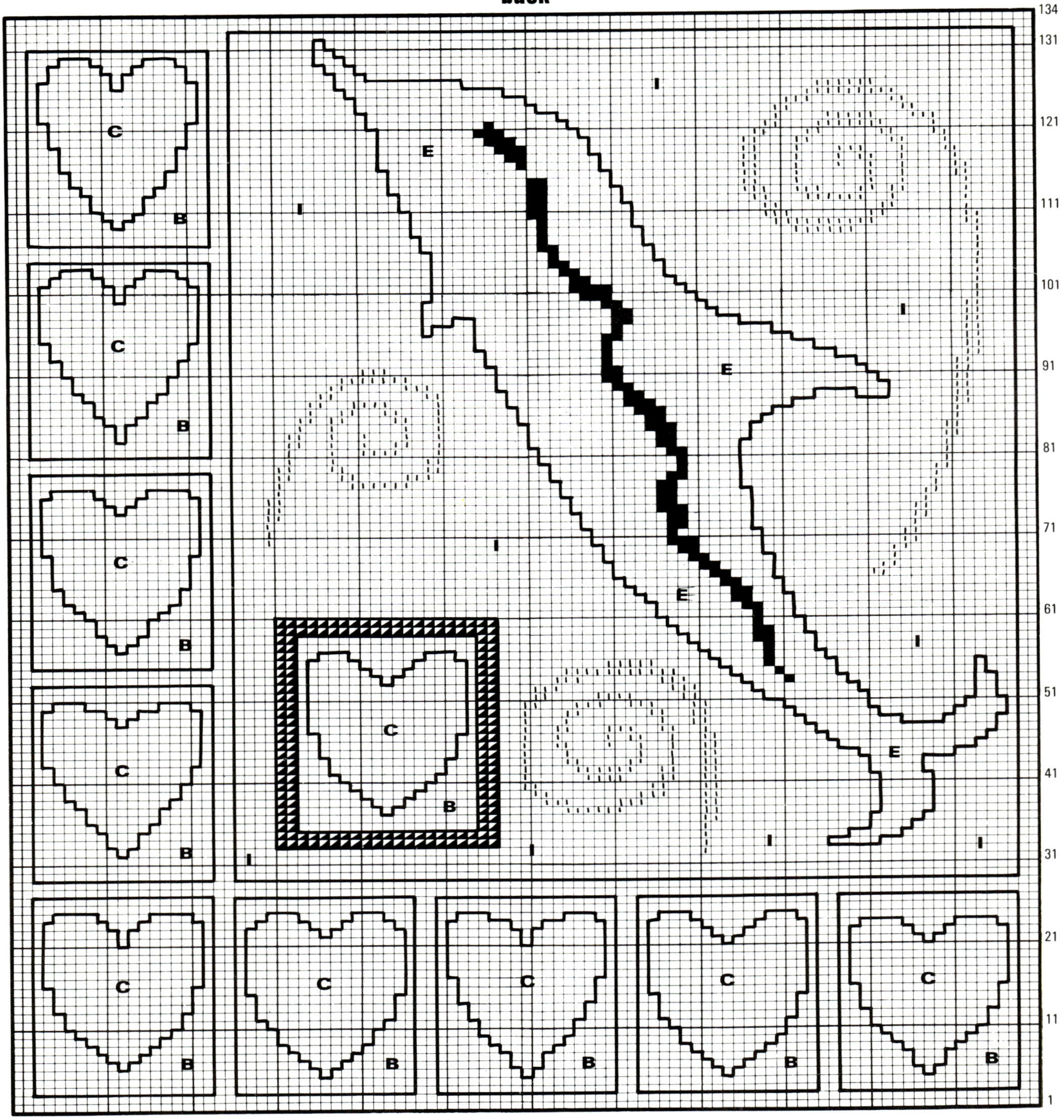

graph 1

sleeves

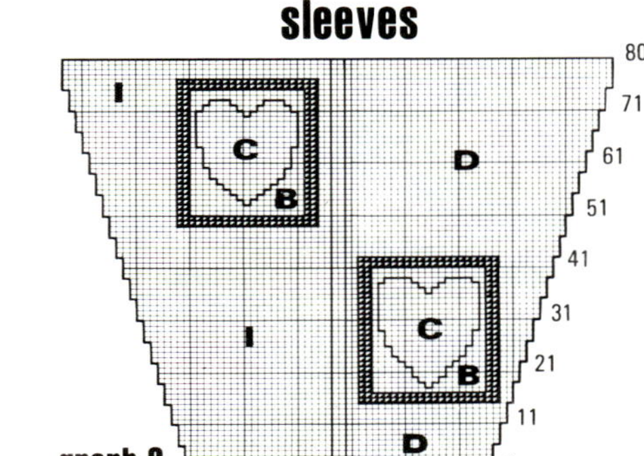

graph 3

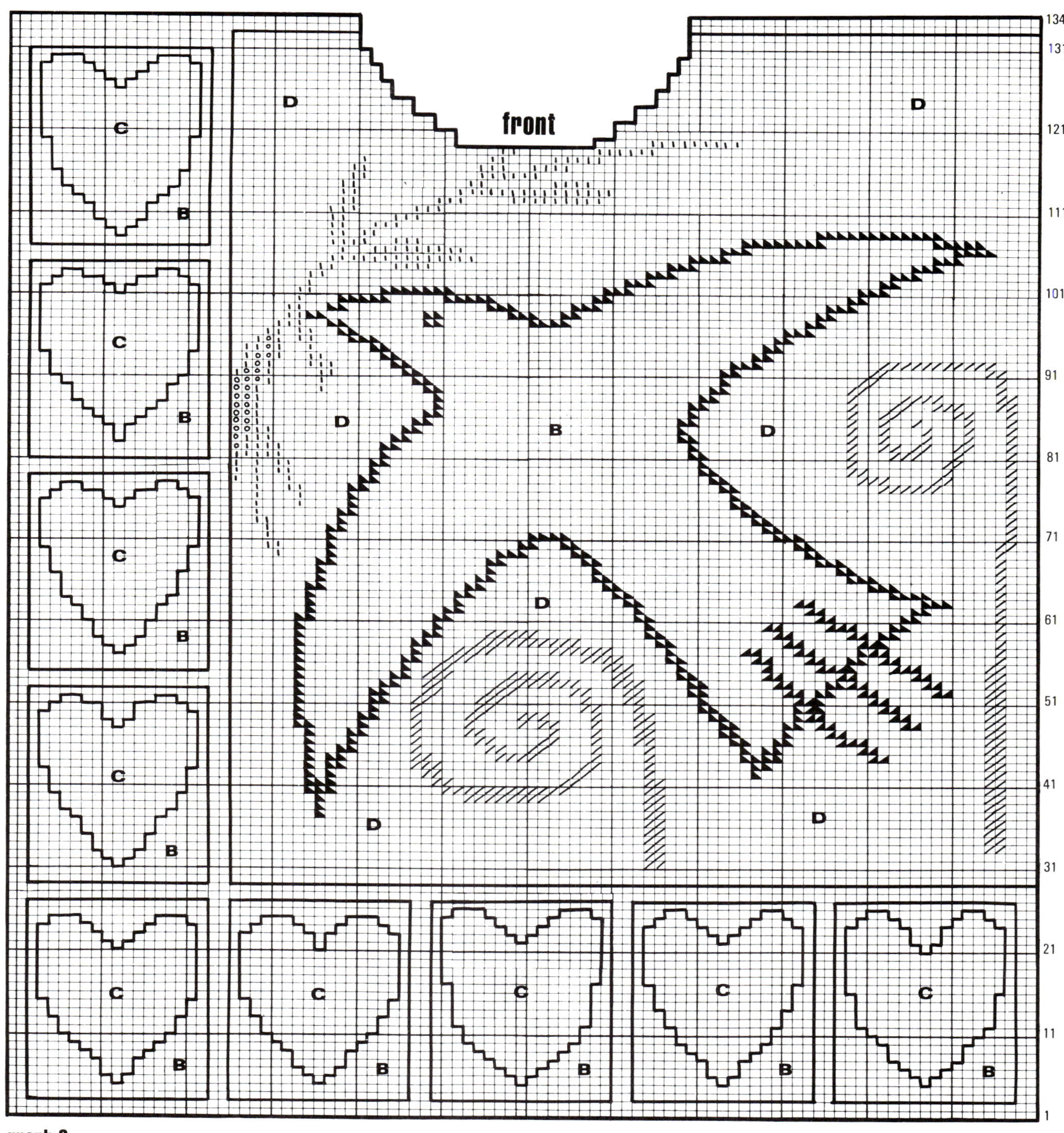

graph 2

KEY
A (Midnight)
B (White)
C (Red)
D (Lavender)
E (Peacock)
F (Black)
G (Regal)
H (Emerald)
I (Peach)
J (Pink)

The hearts and sea-shells symbolise Aphrodite, the goddess of love and the goddess of sea.

MATERIALS
8 colours, see key.
50 g (2 oz) balls of Cleckheaton 5 ply Pure Wool Machine Wash, or equivalent yarn to give stated tension: A 2 balls; B 2 balls; C 2 balls; D 3 balls; E 3 balls; F 2 balls; G 2 balls; H 2 balls.
Pair each of 3.25 mm (No. 10) and 4.00 mm (No. 8) knitting needles. Set of four 3.25 mm (No. 10) knitting needles. 3.00 mm (No. 10) crochet hook.

MEASUREMENTS
Width: 114 cm (45 in)
Length: 64 cm (25 in)
Sleeve seam: 47 cm (18½ in)

TENSION/GAUGE
27 sts and 28 rows to 10 cm (4 in) over colour patt in st st, using 4.00 mm (No. 8) needles. Change needle size if necessary to obtain the correct tension gauge.

BACK
Using 3.25 mm (No. 10) needles and E, cast on 142 sts. Work in K1, P1 rib for 6 cm (2½ in) ending on RS row.
Inc row: K7, * inc 1 st in next st, K8, rep from * to end (157 sts). Change to 4.00 mm (No. 8) needles and st st. Work 162 rows of graph. Cast/bind off.

FRONT
Work as back until 146 rows have been worked.
SHAPE NECK
1st row: Patt 66 sts, cast/bind off centre 25 sts, patt to end.
Cont on last 66 sts, cast off 2 sts at right neck edge on every alt row 5 times, then dec 1 st at neck edge on every foll alt row twice (54 sts rem). Work 2 rows straight. Cast/bind off. Rejoin yarn to left side of neck. Following graph, work to match shaping on right neck side.

KEY
- ☐ **A (Royal Blue)**
- ☒ **B (Turquoise)**
- ⊡ **C (Mauve)**
- ◙ **D (Aqua)**
- ⍁ **E (Coral)**
- ◪ **F (Pink)**
- ◩ **G (Yellow)**
- ⎅ **H (Hot Pink)**
- ☑ **Yellow in garter stitch**

SLEEVES
Both the same.
Using 3.25 mm (No. 10) needles and E, cast on 69 sts. Work in K1, P1 rib for 6 cm (2½ in) ending with RS row.
Inc row: (K3, inc 1 st in next st) 6 times, (K2, inc 1 st in next st) 6 times, (K3, inc 1 st in next st) 6 times, K3 (87 sts).
Change to 4.00 mm (No. 8) needles and st st. Work from graph and inc 1 st each end of 7th row and every foll 6th row 6 times, then every 4th row until there are 135 sts. Cont straight on these sts until 116 rows of graph have been worked, or length req, ending on WS row. Cast/bind off.

EMBROIDERY
Press lightly on wrong side of pieces. Embroider on borders following instructions, then lightly press embroidery.

Border A: Using matching colours and stem stitch outline all hearts and flames.
Band 1: Outline using F shells using stem stitch or chain stitch.
Band 2: Using crochet hook and D, make chain cords and sew them over the words, alternatively embroider in chain stitch.
Band 3: Using crochet hook and H, make chain cords and sew them over the words.
Band 4: Embroider the fine lines on shells, using spliced blue yarn and stem stitch.
Band 5: Outline shells with F, using stem stitch or chain stitch.
Work C2 section in garter stitch, all other sections in st st.

NECKBAND
Sew shoulder seams.
With right side facing, set of four 3.25 mm (No. 10) needles and E, evenly pick up and knit 65 sts on front neck, 49 sts on back neck (114 sts). Work in K1, P1 rib in round until band measures 7.5 cm (3 in). Cast/bind off in rib.

TO FINISH
Place marker on each side edge of back and front at 25 cm (10 in) below shoulder seam. Placing centre of sleeve top to shoulder seams, sew sleeves between markers. Fold neckband in half to inside and loosely stitch down in place. Sew up side and sleeve seams. Press seams open.

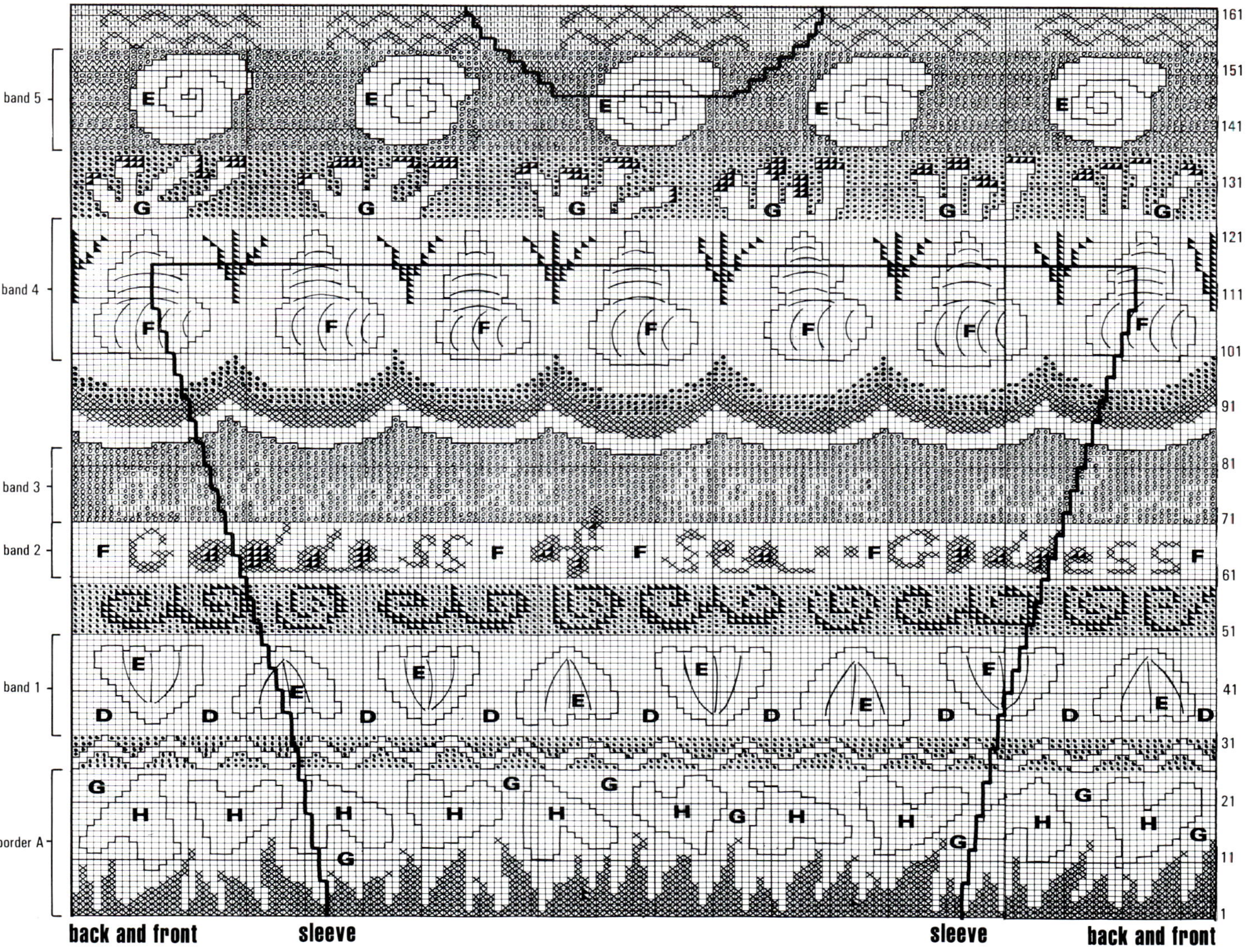
band 5
band 4
band 3
band 2
band 1
border A
161
151
141
131
121
111
101
91
81
71
61
51
41
31
21
11
1
E
G
F
D
H
back and front
sleeve
sleeve
back and front

MATERIALS
16 colours, see key.
50 g (2 oz) balls of Georges Picaud Tricheuse, or equivalent yarn to give stated tension: B 1 ball; F 1 ball; G 6 balls; H 1 ball; I 1 ball; J 1 ball; K 1 ball, O 1 ball.
50 g (2 oz) balls of Georges Picaud 100% Wool 4 Fils, or equivalent yarn to give stated tension: A 2 balls; C 1 ball; D 3 balls; E 2 balls; L 1 ball; M 1 ball; N 1 ball; P 1 ball; small amount of black wool for embroidery.
Pair each 3.75 mm (No. 9) and 3.25 mm (No. 10) knitting needles. Set of four 3.00 mm (No. 11) knitting needles.

MEASUREMENTS
(Garment Measures)
Bust: 115 cm (45 in)
Length: 71 cm (28 in)
Sleeve seam: 46 cm (18 in)

TENSION/GAUGE
23½ sts and 29 rows to 10 cm (4 in) over st st in picture knit, using 3.75 mm (No. 9) needles. Change needle size if necessary to obtain the stated tension/gauge.

BACK
With 3.25 mm (No. 10) needles and G, cast on 119 sts. Work in K1, P1 rib for 6 cm (2½ in), ending on RS row.
Inc row: Rib 2 sts, (inc 1 st in next st, rib 5 sts) 20 times, ending with rib 2 sts instead of 5 sts (139 sts).
Change to 3.75 mm (No. 9) needles and st st. Work 110 rows from graph 1.

This is a celebration of my most loved Australian symbols in brilliant dancing colour: the koala, the boomerang, the emu, the kangaroo, the gumleaf, the wattle, Sturt's desert pea, the Opera House.

SHAPE ARMHOLES
Cont to work from graph 1, cast/bind off 5 sts at beg of next 2 rows, then dec 1 st each end of every row 10 times (109 sts rem) *. Cont straight for 66 rows. Cast/bind off loosely.

FRONT
Work as for back to *. Cont straight for 42 rows.
SHAPE NECK
Next row: Work 44 sts from graph, cast/bind off centre 21 sts loosely, work to end.
Cont on last 44 sts for right side of neck. ** Dec 1 st at neck edge on every row 5 times, then on every alt row 7 times (32 sts rem).
Work 4 rows straight. Cast/bind off loosely. Ret to rem 44 sts, rejoin yarn at left neck edge and work as other side from ** to end. Cast/bind off loosely.

SLEEVES
Both the same.
With 3.25 mm (No. 10) needles and G, cast on 57 sts. Work in K1, P1 rib for 6 cm (2½ in), ending on RS row.
Inc row: Rib 2 sts, (inc 1 st in next st, rib 3 sts) 14 times, ending with rib 2 sts instead of 3 sts (71 sts).
Change to 3.75 mm (No. 9) needles and st st. Working from graph 2 inc 1 st each end of 11th row once, then on every foll 6th row 7 times, then on every foll 4th row 15 times (117 sts). Work 3 rows straight.
SHAPE TOP
Cont from graph 2, cast/bind off 5 sts at beg of next 2 rows, then dec 1 st each end of next 10 rows (87 sts rem). Cast/bind off loosely.

NECKBAND
Sew in all ends. Sew shoulder seams. With set of four 3.00 mm (No. 11) needles and G, pick up and knit 69 sts on front neck, 47 sts on back neck (116 sts). Work in rnds of K1, P1 rib for 8 cm (3¼ in). Cast/bind off ribwise loosely.

TO FINISH
Sew up side seams, then sleeve seams. Sew sleeves evenly into armholes. Fold neckband in half to inside and stitch loosely in place.

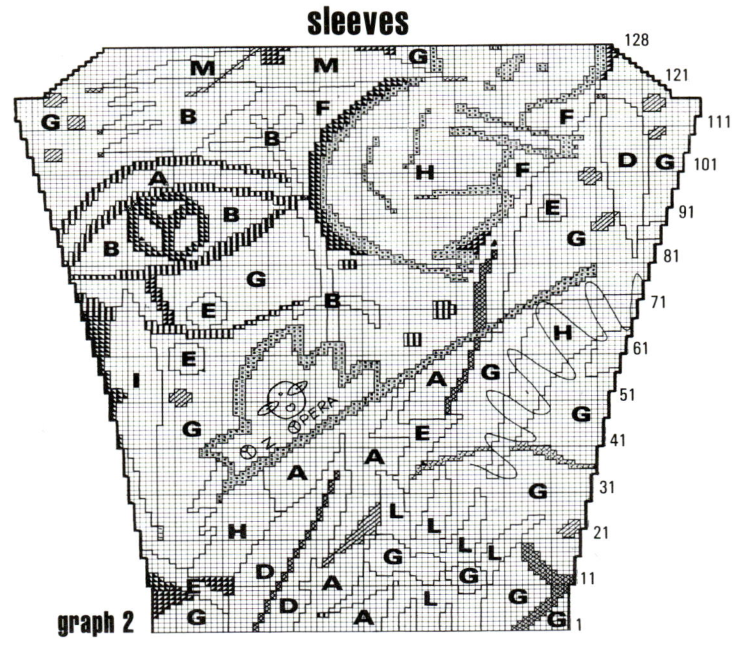

front and back

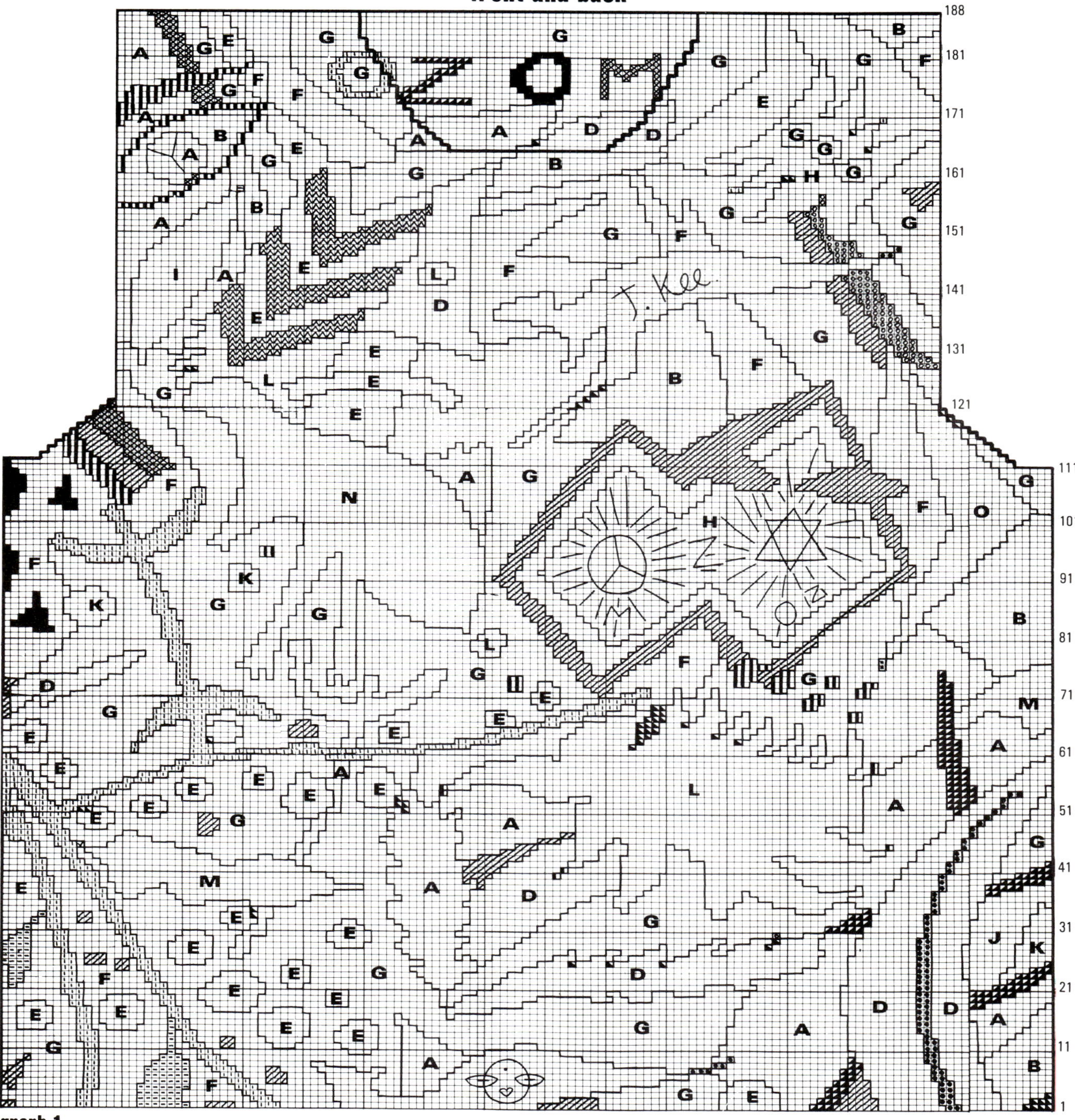

graph 1

KEY

- A (Aqua)
- B (Pink)
- C (Cream)
- D (Bright Green)
- E (Yellow)
- F (Purple)
- G (Black)
- H (Light Red)
- I (Green 1)
- J (Orange)
- K (Fuschia)
- L (Dark Red)
- M (Green 2)
- N (Violet)
- O (Royal Blue)
- P (Grey)

Using garter and stem stitch embroider as illustrated.

WARATAH AND BLACKBOY

MATERIALS

16 colours, see key.
50 g (2 oz) balls of Georges Picaud Tricheuse, or equivalent yarn to give stated tension: A 2 balls; B 1 ball; C 1 ball; D 1 ball; E 1 ball; F 2 balls; G 2 balls; I 1 ball; J 1 ball; P 1 ball.
50 g (2 oz) balls of Georges Picaud 100% Wool 4 Fils, or equivalent yarn to give stated tension: H 1 ball; K 1 ball; L 1 ball; M 1 ball; N 1 ball; O 1 ball; small amount of black wool for embroidery.
Pair each 3.75 mm (No. 9) and 3.25 mm (No. 10) knitting needles. Set of four 3.00 mm (No. 11) knitting needles.

MEASUREMENTS
(Garment Measures)

Bust: 119 cm (47 in)
Length: 71 cm (28 in)
Sleeve seam: 46 cm (18 in)

TENSION/GAUGE

23 sts and 29 rows to 10 cm (4 in) over st st in picture knit, using 3.75 mm (No. 9) needles. Change needle size if necessary to obtain the stated tension/gauge.

BACK

With 3.25 mm (No. 10) needles and C, cast on 119 sts. Work in K1, P1 rib for 6 cm (2½ in), ending with RS row.
Inc row: Rib 2 sts, (inc 1 st in next st, rib 5 sts) 20 times, ending with rib 2 sts instead of 5 sts (139 sts).
Change to 3.75 mm (No. 9) needles and st st. Work 188 rows of graph 1. Cast/bind off loosely.

This is the perfect symbol in nature of destruction and regeneration. For out of the bushfire comes the waratah and the 'blackboy'.

FRONT

Work as for back until 164 rows of graph 1 have been worked.

SHAPE NECK

Next row: Work 59 sts from graph, cast/bind off centre 21 sts loosely, work from graph to end.
Cont on last 59 sts for right side of neck.
* Dec 1 st at neck edge on every row 5 times, then on every alt row 7 times (47 sts rem). Work 6 rows straight. Cast/bind off loosely.
Ret to rem 59 sts, rejoin yarn at left neck edge and work as other side from * to end.
Cast/bind off loosely.

LEFT SLEEVE

With 3.25 mm (No. 10) needles and C, cast on 57 sts. Work in K1, P1 rib for 6 cm (2½ in), ending on RS row.
Inc row: Rib 2 sts, (inc 1 st in next st, rib 3 sts) 14 times, ending with rib 2 sts instead of 3 sts (71 sts).
Change to 3.75 mm (No. 9) needles and st st. Working from graph 2 inc 1 st each end of 11th row once, then on every foll 6th row 7 times, then on every foll 4th row 15 times (117 sts). Work 3 rows straight from graph. Cast/bind off loosely.

RIGHT SLEEVE

Work as for left sleeve but reading from graph 3.

TO MAKE UP

Sew in all ends. Press lightly on wrong sides. Sew shoulder seams.

NECKBAND

With set of four 3.00 mm (No. 11) needles and C, pick up and knit 69 sts on front neck, 47 sts on back neck (116 sts). Work in rnds of K1, P1 rib for 8 cm (3¼ in). Cast/bind off ribwise loosely.

OPTIONAL EMBROIDERY

Embroidered line motifs marked on graph may be worked stem stitch in black wool. Knot motifs may be worked in yellow French knots before finishing off garment.

TO FINISH

Matching centre of sleeve top to shoulder seams, sew sleeves in place, then sew up side and sleeve seams. Fold neckband in half to inside and stitch down loosely.

left sleeve

graph 2

right sleeve

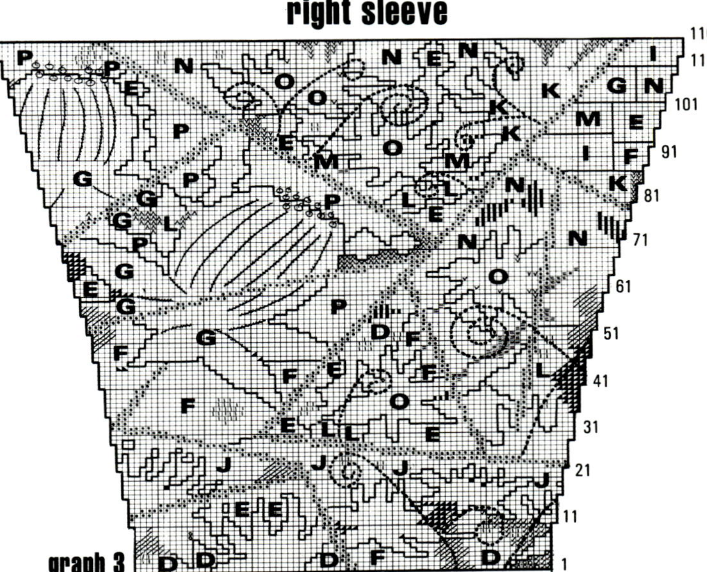

graph 3

front and back

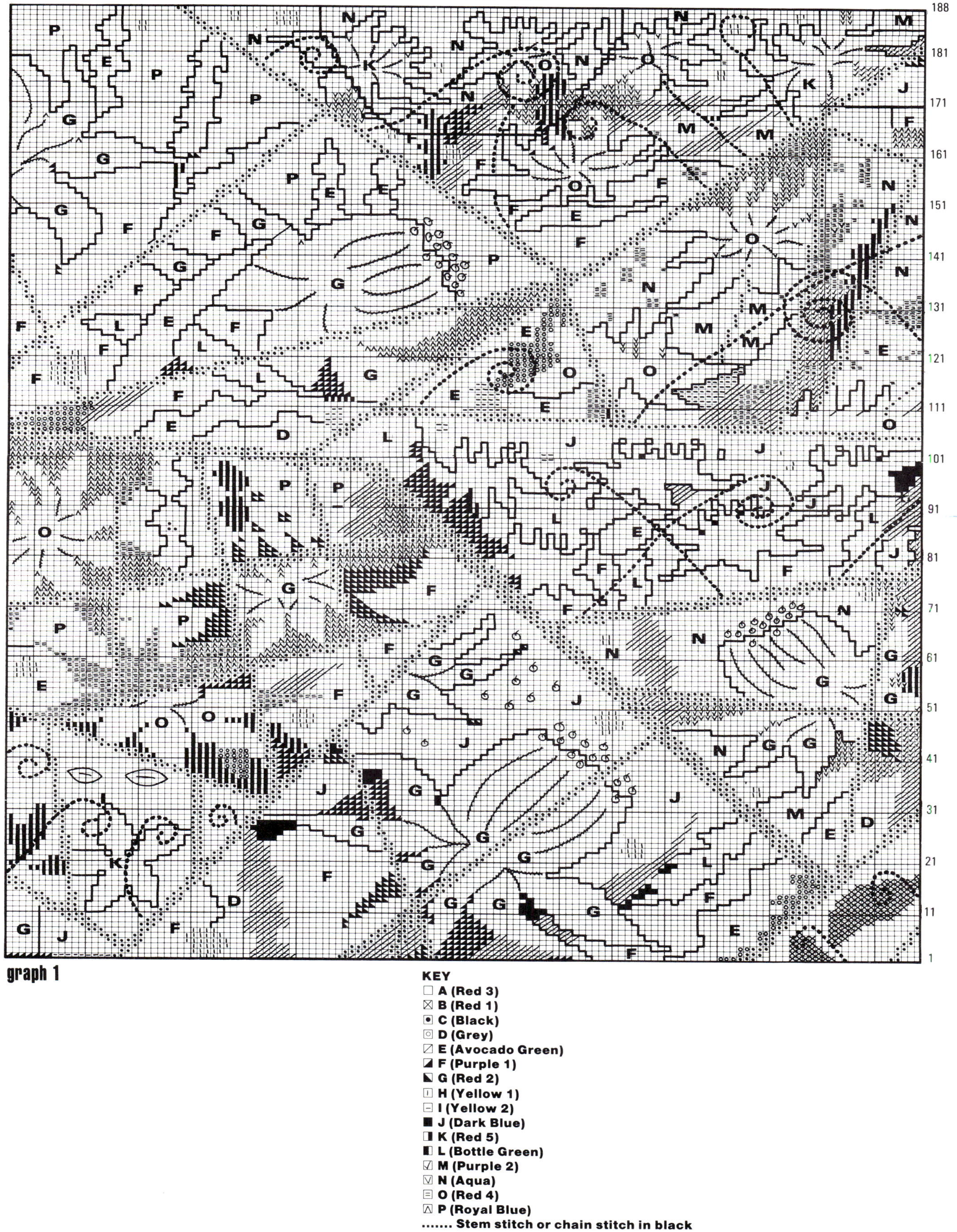

graph 1

KEY

- ☐ A (Red 3)
- ☒ B (Red 1)
- C (Black)
- D (Grey)
- E (Avocado Green)
- F (Purple 1)
- G (Red 2)
- H (Yellow 1)
- I (Yellow 2)
- J (Dark Blue)
- K (Red 5)
- L (Bottle Green)
- M (Purple 2)
- N (Aqua)
- O (Red 4)
- P (Royal Blue)
- .... Stem stitch or chain stitch in black
- Stem stitch in black
- French knot in same shade of red as flower or yellow

MATERIALS

7 colours, see key.
50 g (2 oz) balls of Cleckheaton 8 ply Caprice Mohair, or equivalent yarn to give stated tension: A 8; B 2; C 2; D 1; E 2; F 1; G 2 balls.
Pair each 4.50 mm (No. 7) and 3.25 mm (No. 10) knitting needles. Set of four 3.25 mm (No. 10) knitting needles.

MEASUREMENTS
(Garment Measures)

Bust: 127 cm (50 in)
Length: 71 cm (28 in)
Sleeve seam: 46 cm (18 in)

TENSION/GAUGE

22 sts and 24 rows to 10 cm (4 in) over st st in picture knit, using 4.50 mm (No. 7) needles. Change needle size if necessary to obtain the stated tension/gauge.

BACK

With 3.25 mm (No. 10) needles and A, cast on 121 sts. Work in K1, P1 rib for 6 cm (2½ in), ending with RS row.
Inc row: (rib 4 sts, inc 1 st in next st) twice, (rib 5 sts, inc 1 st in next st) 16 times, rib 5 sts, (inc 1 st in next st, rib 4 sts) twice, (141 sts). Change to 4.50 mm (No. 7) needles and st st. Work 148 rows of graph 1.

SHAPE NECK

Next row: Work 52 sts from graph, cast/bind off centre 37 sts loosely, work to end of row. Cont on last 52 sts from graph for left side of neck and cast/bind off at beg of every alt row 2 sts 3 times (46 sts rem). Work 1 row as on graph. Cast/bind off loosely.
Ret to rem 52 sts, rejoin yarn at right neck edge. Working from graph, cast/bind off at beg of next and every foll alt row 2 sts 3 times in all (46 sts rem). Work 2 rows as on graph. Cast/bind off loosely.

The multitude of colours, shapes and patterns of Australia's native flowers are a constant source of inspiration to me. The wattle, waratah, flannel flower, kangaroo paw and Sturt's desert pea are my favourite flowers in nature.

FRONT

Work as for back until 130 rows of graph 1 have been worked.

SHAPE NECK

Next row: Work 60 sts from graph, cast/bind off centre 21 sts loosely, work to end of row. Cont on last 60 sts from graph for right side of neck. Cast/bind off at beg of every alt row 2 sts 5 times, then 1 st 4 times (46 sts rem). Work 7 rows straight as on graph. Cast/bind off loosely.
Ret to rem 60 sts, rejoin yarn at left neck edge. Work from graph for left side of neck and cast/bind off at beg of next and every foll alt row 2 sts 5 times, then 1 st 4 times (46 sts rem). Work 8 rows straight as on graph. Cast/bind off loosely.

LEFT SLEEVE

With 3.25 mm (No. 10) needles and A, cast on 55 sts. Work in K1, P1 rib for 6 cm (2½ in), ending with RS row.
Inc row: Rib 6 sts, (inc 1 st in next st, rib 5 sts) 8 times, rib 1 st, (63 sts). Change to 4.50 mm (No. 7) needles and st st. Work from graph 2 at same time inc 1 st each end of 5th row once, then inc 1 st each end of foll alt row once, then on foll 4th row once. Rep last 6 rows until there are 119 sts, then inc 1 st each end of foll 4th row once (121 sts). Work 7 rows straight as on graph. Cast/bind off loosely.

RIGHT SLEEVE

Work as for left sleeve but following graph 3.

TO MAKE UP

Sew in all ends. Press lightly on wrong sides. Sew shoulder seams.

NECKBAND

With set of four 3.25 mm (No. 10) needles and A, evenly pick up and knit 73 sts on front neck, 55 sts on back neck (128 sts). Work in rnds of K1, P1 rib for 13 cm (5 in). Cast/bind off loosely.

TO FINISH

Matching centre of sleeve top to shoulder seam, sew sleeves evenly in position, then sew up side and sleeve seams. Fold neckband in half to inside and loosely stitch down in place.

left sleeve

graph 2

front and back

graph 1

KEY

- ☐ A (Jacaranda)
- ☒ B (Cerise)
- ⊡ C (Jade)
- ◎ D (White)
- ▨ E (Yellow)
- ◪ F (Black)
- ◩ G (Light Red)

right sleeve

96
91
81
71
61
51
41
31
21
11
1

graph 3

PAX JOY CARDIGAN

MATERIALS

11 colours, see key.
50 g (2 oz) balls of Cleckheaton 5 ply Pure Wool Machine Wash, or equivalent yarn to give stated tension: A 2 balls; B 2 balls; C 2 balls; D 2 balls; E 2 balls; F 2 balls; G 2 balls; H 2 balls; I 4 balls; J 2 balls; K 1 ball.
Pair each of 4.00 mm (No. 8) and 3.00 mm (No. 11) knitting needles. 3.00 mm (No. 10) crochet hook. 6 buttons.

MEASUREMENTS (Garment Measures)

Bust: 118 cm (46½ in)
Length: 67 cm (26½ in)
Sleeve seam: 50 cm (19½ in)

TENSION/GAUGE

27 sts and 29 rows to 10 cm (4 in) over st st in fair isle patt, using 4.00 mm (No. 8) needles. Change needle size if necessary to obtain the stated tension/gauge.

BACK

Work as for back of Pax Joy Jumper, beg at 1st row instead of 45th row of graph.

LEFT FRONT

With 3.00 mm (No. 11) needles and I, cast on 93 sts. Work in K1, P1 rib for 6 cm (2½ in), ending with WS row.
Next row: With 4.00 mm (No. 8) needles, work 1st row of graph for left front as shown over 1st 74 sts, leave rem 19 sts on a safety pin for front band. Beg with 2nd row, cont to work from graph until 98th row has been worked.

SHAPE NECK

Cont from the graph and dec 1 st at neck edge on next row, then on every alt row until 61 sts rem, then on every foll 4th row until 50 sts rem. Work straight on these rem sts until 172 rows of graph have been worked. Cast/bind off.

RIGHT FRONT

Work as for left front until rib band measures 2 cm (¾ in) from beg, ending with WS row.
Buttonhole row: Rib 8 sts, cast/bind off 4 sts, rib to end.
Next row: Rib and cast on 4 sts over cast/bind off 4 sts.
Cont in rib until band measures 6 cm (2½ in) from beg, ending with RS row.
Next row: Rib to last 19 sts, leave rem 19 sts on a safety pin for front band.

This is my ultimate peace design. It is a celebration of the symbols of peace, joy and nature: fern fronds and gumleaves for the wilderness, the rainbow serpent for Aboriginal Dreaming, butterflies for freedom, waratahs for fire and earth, dolphins for the sea, peace and love.

KEY
□ **A (Red)**
⊠ **B (Yellow)**
▣ **C (Pink)**
◎ **D (Mid Blue)**
◪ **E (Mauve)**
◩ **F (Black)**
◣ **G (White)**
◫ **H (Green)**
⊟ **I (Royal Blue)**
■ **J (Turquoise)**
◨ **K (Salmon)**
Note: Graph is not marked for Skirt decreases. See text.

Change to 4.00 mm (No. 8) needles and st st. Work from graph for right front and shape neck to match left front.

SLEEVES

Work as for sleeves of Pax Joy Jumper.

OPTIONAL EMBROIDERY

Press lightly on wrong sides. Embroider outline of motifs in stem stitch or crochet chain chords and sew over outlines. Lightly press embroidery. Sew shoulder seams.

Band 1: Outline in E
Band 2: Outline in F
Band 3: Motif in H
Band 4: Outline in F
Band 5: Outline in C
Band 6: Outline in E
Band 7: Outline in F
Band 8: Motif in C
Band 9: Centres in B
Band 10: Centres in F
Band 11: Outline in C

LEFT FRONT AND NECKBAND

Return to 19 sts for front band, with rs facing and 3.00 mm (No. 11) needles, join I to 1st st, inc 1 st in 1st st and work in rib to end (20 sts). Cont in rib until band, when slightly stretched, fits along front of cardigan and along back neck to centre. Cast/bind off ribwise.

SIX BUTTONHOLE POSITIONS

First buttonhole is already made. On body of cardigan, mark placing of 6th buttonhole at 1 cm (⅜ in) below the beg of front neck shaping and 4 others evenly spaced between this and lowest one. Buttonholes will be approximately 24 rows apart.

TO MAKE A BUTTONHOLE

On RS row at each marker, work 8 sts in rib, cast/bind off centre 4 sts, rib to end. On next row work in rib as before and cast on 4 sts at centre.

RIGHT FRONT AND NECKBAND

With ws facing work as left front and neckband with addition of making buttonholes as given.

TO MAKE UP

Join two bands tog at centre back neck, then sew bands in place. Matching centre of sleeve top to shoulder seam, sew sleeves in place, then sew up side and sleeve seams. Sew on buttons.

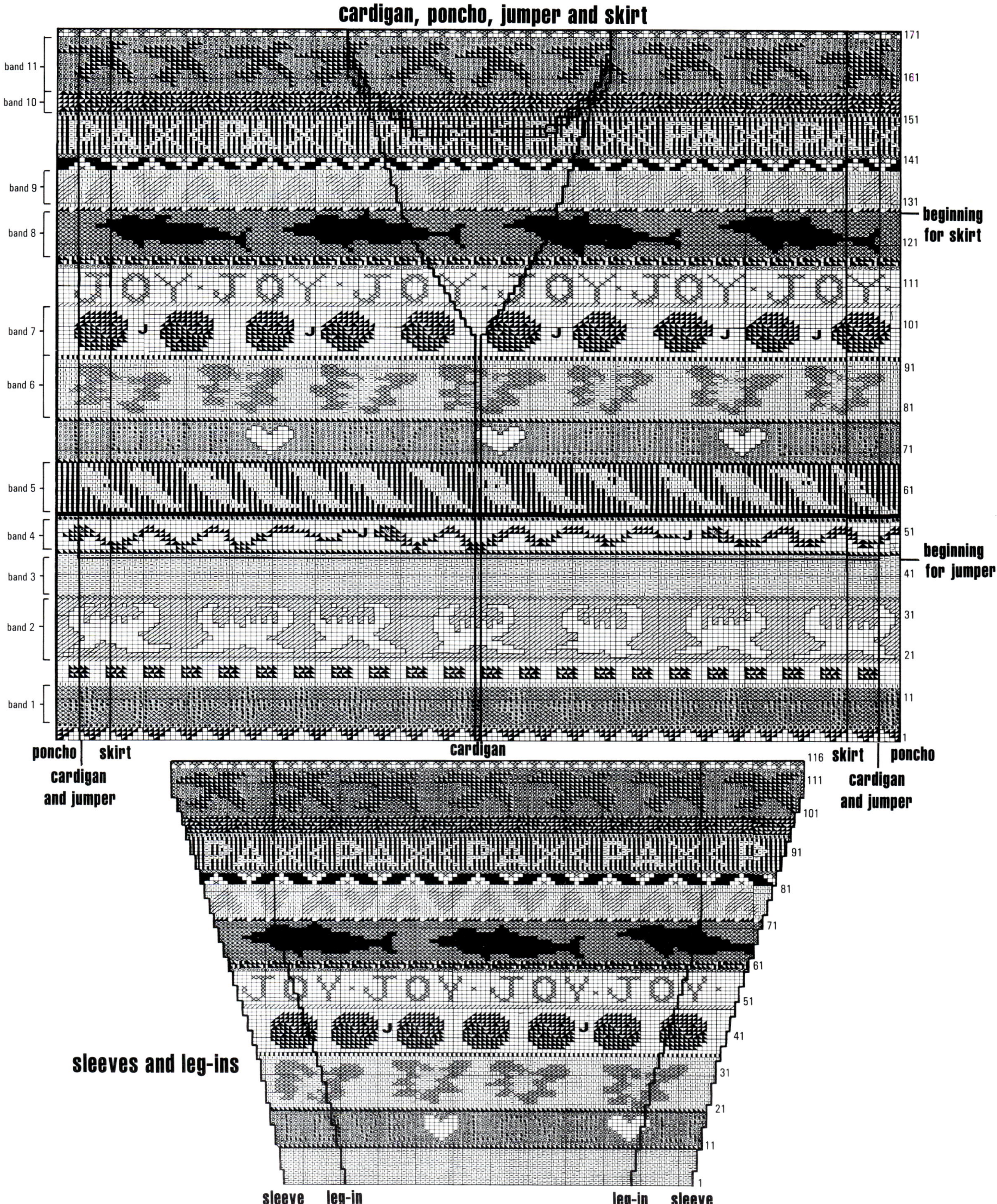
cardigan, poncho, jumper and skirt
band 11
band 10
band 9
band 8
band 7
band 6
band 5
band 4
band 3
band 2
band 1
171
161
151
141
131
121
111
101
91
81
71
61
51
41
31
21
11
1
beginning for skirt
beginning for jumper
poncho
cardigan and jumper
skirt
cardigan
skirt
poncho
cardigan and jumper
116
111
101
91
81
71
61
51
41
31
21
11
1
sleeves and leg-ins
sleeve
leg-in
leg-in
sleeve

PAX JOY

PAX JOY SKIRT

MATERIALS
11 colours, see key.
50 g (2 oz) balls of Cleckheaton 5 ply Pure Wool Machine Wash, or equivalent yarn to give stated tension: A 1 ball; B 1 ball; C 1 ball; D 2 balls; E 1 ball; F 1 ball; G 1 ball; H 1 ball; I 2 balls; J 1 ball; K1 ball.
Pair each 4.00 mm (No. 8) and 3.00 mm (No. 11) knitting needles. Elastic.

MEASUREMENTS
(Garment Measures)
Length including folded waistband: 71 cm (28 in)
Lower edge: 102 cm (40 in)

TENSION/GAUGE
26½ sts and 28 rows to 10 cm (4 in) over st st in fair isle patt, using 4.00 mm (No. 8) needles. Change needle size if necessary to obtain the stated tension/gauge.

BACK AND FRONT ALIKE
With 3.00 mm (No. 11) needles and I, cast on 137 sts. Work in K1, P1 rib for 6 cm (2½ in), ending with WS row. Change to 4.00 mm (No. 8) needles and st st. Work from graph as marked for skirt but beg at 129th row and work to the end of graph (44 rows), then return to 1st row of graph and cont to work until 84th row has been worked. Cont to work from graph, beg at 85th row of graph and dec 1 st each end of next and every foll 6th row 7 times more (121 sts rem), then work 1 row without dec, ending with 128th row of graph. (Note: skirt decreases are not marked on graph.) There should be 172 rows of fair isle patt. Change to 3.00 mm (No. 11) needles. Cont with D only and work in K1, P1 rib for 6 cm (2½ in). Cast/bind off in rib loosely.

TO MAKE UP
Press lightly on wrong sides. Sew in all ends. Sew up side seams. Cut elastic to fit around waist firmly. Fold waistband in half to inside and loosely stitch down in place, leaving about 5 cm (2 in) open. Thread elastic through waistband, sew ends of elastic together. Stitch down remaining 5 cm (2 in) of waistband.

PAX JOY JUMPER

MATERIALS
11 colours, see key.
50 g (2 oz) balls of Cleckheaton 5 ply Pure Wool Machine Wash, or equivalent yarn to give stated tension: A 1 ball; B 2 balls; C 1 ball; D 2 balls; E 1 ball; F 1 ball; G 2 balls; H 2 balls; I 2 balls; J 2 balls; K 1 ball.
Pair each 4.00 mm (No. 8) and 3.00 mm (No. 11) knitting needles. Set of four 3.00 mm (No. 11) knitting needles.

MEASUREMENTS
(Garment Measures)
Bust: 108 cm (42½ in)
Length: 51 cm (20 in)
Sleeve seam: 46 cm (18 in)

TENSION/GAUGE
27 sts and 28 rows to 10 cm (4 in) over st st in fair isle patt, using 4.00 mm (No. 8) needles. Change needle size if necessary to obtain the stated tension/gauge.

BACK
With 3.00 mm (No. 11) needles and I, cast on 135 sts. Work in K1, P1 rib for 5 cm (2 in), ending with RS row.
Inc row: Rib 9 sts, (inc 1 st in next st, rib 8 sts) rep to end (149 sts). Change to 4.00 mm (No. 8) needles and st st. Work from graph as marked for short sweater, *beg at 45th row* *. Cont to work to the end of the graph. There should be 128 rows above rib band. Cast/bind off loosely.

FRONT
Work as for back to *. Cont to work until 146th row of graph has been worked. There should be 102 rows above rib band at this point.

SHAPE NECK
Next row: Work 62 sts from graph, cast/bind off centre 25 sts, work from graph to end. Cont on last 62 sts from graph for right side of neck and cast/bind off at neck edge on every 2nd row 2 sts 5 times, then 1 st twice (50 sts rem). Work 11 rows straight from graph. Cast/bind off.
Ret to rem 62 sts, rejoin yarn at neck edge. Work from graph for left side of neck and cast/bind off at neck edge on next and every foll 2nd row 2 sts 5 times, then 1 st twice. Work 12 rows straight from graph. Cast/bind off.

SLEEVES
With 3.00 mm (No. 11) needles and I, cast on 69 sts. Work in K1, P1 rib for 5 cm (2 in), ending with RS row.
Inc row: (K3, inc 1 st in next st) 6 times, (K2, inc 1 st in next st) 6 times, (K3, inc 1 st in next st) 6 times, K3 (87 sts).
Change to 4.00 mm (No. 8) needles and st st. Work from graph for sleeves of cardigan and inc 1 st each end of 5th row once, then on every foll 6th row 5 times more, then on every foll 4th row until there are 135 sts. Cont on these sts until 116 rows of graph have been worked. Cast/bind off.

TO MAKE UP
Press lightly on wrong sides. Sew in all ends. Sew shoulder seams.

NECKBAND
With set of four 3.00 mm (No. 11) needles and I, pick up and knit 77 sts on front neck, 53 sts on back neck (130 sts). Work in rnds of K1, P1 rib for 6 cm (2½ in). Cast/bind off ribwise loosely. Fold band in half to inside and stitch down in place.

TO FINISH
Matching centre of sleeve top to shoulder seam, join sleeves in place, then sew up side and sleeve seams.

PAX JOY LEG-INS

MATERIALS
11 colours, see key.
Note: These quantities may vary.
50 g (2 oz) balls of Cleckheaton 5 ply Pure Wool Machine Wash, or equivalent yarn to give stated tension: A 1 ball; B 1 ball; C 1 ball; D 1 ball; E 1 ball; F 1 ball; G 1 ball; H 1 ball; I 2 balls; J 1 ball; K 1 ball.
Pair each 4.00 mm (No. 8) and 3.25 mm (No. 10) knitting needles.

MEASUREMENTS
Width above lower rib band: 22 cm (8¾ in)
Width below top rib band: 33 cm (13 in)
Total length: 66 cm (26 in)

TENSION/GAUGE
27 sts and 29 rows to 10 cm (4 in) over st st in fair isle patt, using 4.00 mm (No. 8) needles. Change needle size if necessary to obtain the stated tension/gauge.

LEG-INS
Work two, both the same.
With 3.25 mm (No. 10) needles and I, *loosely* cast on 61 sts. Work in K1, P1 rib for 13 cm (5 in), ending with WS row. Change to 4.00 mm (No. 8) needles and st st. Work from graph marked for leg-ins (on the graph for sleeves of jumper) and inc 1 st each end of 5th row once, then on every foll 6th row 4 times more, then on every foll 4th row 10 times (91 sts). Cont straight on these sts until 116 rows of graph have been worked, then change to 3.25 mm (No. 10) needles and I, work in rib as before for 13 cm (5 in). Loosely cast/bind off in rib.

TO MAKE UP
Press lightly on wrong sides. Sew in all ends. Sew seams, matching patt borders.

PAX JOY PONCHO

MATERIALS
11 colours, see key.
50 g (2 oz) balls of Cleckheaton 8 ply Caprice Mohair, or equivalent yarn to give stated tension: A 2 balls; B 3 balls; E 1 ball; F 2 balls; H 2 balls.
50 g (2 oz) balls of Cleckheaton 8 ply Pure Wool, or equivalent yarn to give stated tension: C 1 ball; D 2 balls; G 2 balls; I 5 balls; J 2 balls; K 2 balls.
Pair each 5.00 mm (No. 6) and 3.75 mm (No. 9) knitting needles. Set of four 3.25 mm (No. 10) knitting needles. One long 3.75 mm (No. 9) circular needle.

MEASUREMENTS
Width: 77 cm (30¼ in)
Length: 73 cm (29 in)

TENSION/GAUGE
22 sts and 24 rows to 10 cm (4 in) over st st in fair isle patt, using 5.00 mm (No. 6) needles. Change needle size if necessary to obtain the stated tension/gauge.

BACK
With 3.75 mm (No. 9) needles and I, cast on 157 sts. Work 10 rows in st st. Purl 1 row for hem line. Beg with purl row work 11 rows in st st. Change to 5.00 mm (No. 6) needles and work 172 rows in st st from graph.
Cast/bind off.

FRONT
Work as for back until 148 rows of graph have been worked.
SHAPE NECK
Next row: Work 66 sts from graph, cast/bind off centre 25 sts, work from graph to end.
Cont on last 66 sts from graph for right side of neck and cast/bind off at beg of every 2nd row 2 sts 4 times, then 1 st 4 times (54 sts rem). Cont on these rem sts straight from graph for further 8 rows. Cast/bind off.
Ret to rem 66 sts, rejoin yarn at neck edge. Cast/bind off at beg of next and every foll 2nd row 2 sts 4 times, then 1 st 4 times. Cont on rem 54 sts for further 9 rows from graph. Cast/bind off.

SIDE BORDERS
Join shoulder seams. With rs facing and a long 3.75 mm (No. 9) circular needle and I, beg and end at hem line, evenly pick up and knit 335 sts on side edge. Beg with purl row work 10 rows in st st. Knit 1 row for hem line. Work 10 rows more in st st. Cast/bind off. Work the same for other side edge.

NECKBAND
With rs facing and set of four 3.25 mm (No. 10) needles and I, evenly pick up and knit 70 sts on front neck, 54 sts on back neck (124 sts). Work in rnds of K1, P1 rib for 6 cm (2½ in). Cast/bind off ribwise loosely.

TO FINISH
Press lightly. Sew in all ends. Fold hems to wrong side and stitch down, then close ends of hems. Fold neckband in half to inside and loosely stitch down.

PAX VEST

MATERIALS
7 colours, see key.
50 g (2 oz) balls of Cleckheaton 8 ply Pure Wool Machine Wash, or equivalent yarn to give stated tension: A 5 balls; B 3 balls; C 2 balls; D 4 balls; E 2 balls; F 2 balls; G 1 ball.
Pair each 4.50 mm (No. 7) and 3.25 mm (No. 10) knitting needles. 6 buttons.

MEASUREMENTS (Garment Measures)
Bust: 130 cm (51 in)
Length: 61 cm (24 in)

TENSION/GAUGE
23 sts and 27 rows to 10 cm (4 in) over st st in fair isle patt, using 4.50 mm (No. 7) needles. Change needle size if necessary to obtain the stated tension/gauge.

BACK
With 3.25 mm (No. 10) needles and A, cast on 135 sts.
1st row: K1, (P1, K1 tbl) rep to last 2 sts, P1, K1.
2nd row: P1, (K1 tbl, P1) rep to end.
Rep last 2 rows for rib patt until 6 cm (2¼ in), ending with RS row.
Inc row: Rib 7 sts, (inc 1 st in next st, rib 7 sts) rep 16 times in all (151 sts).
Change to 4.50 mm (No. 7) needles and st st. Follow graph until 80 rows have been worked.

SHAPE ARMHOLES
Continuing from graph, cast/bind off at beg of next and every row 8 sts twice, 2 sts 8 times, then dec 1 st each end of next and every foll alt row 4 times in all (111 sts rem). Cont on these rem 111 sts until 152 rows of graph have been worked. Cast/bind off.

LEFT FRONT
With 3.25 mm (No. 10) needles and A, cast on 67 sts. Work in rib as for back for 6 cm (2¼ in), ending with RS row.
Inc row: Rib 5 sts, (inc 1 st in next st, rib 7 sts) rep 8 times in all but ending with rib 5 sts instead of 7 sts (75 sts).
Change to 4.50 mm (No. 7) needles and st st. Work from graph marked for left front until 80 rows have been worked.

SHAPE ARMHOLE AND NECK
Continuing from graph, cast/bind off at beg of next and each alt row 8 sts once, 2 sts 4 times, then dec 1 st at same edge on next and every alt row 4 times *at same time* dec 1 st at front edge on next row, then on every foll alt row 7 times more, then on every foll 4th row 12 times (35 sts rem). Work 9 rows straight from graph. Cast/bind off.

RIGHT FRONT
Work as for left front but from graph marked for right front until 81 rows of graph have been worked.

SHAPE ARMHOLE AND NECK
Continuing from graph as before, cast/bind off at beg of next and every foll alt row 8 sts once, 2 sts 4 times, then dec 1 st at same edge on next and every alt row 4 times *at same time* dec 1 st at front edge on next and every foll alt row 8 times, then every foll 4th row 12 times. Work 8 rows straight from graph. Cast/bind off.

TO MAKE UP
Press lightly on wrong sides. Sew in all ends securely. Sew shoulder seams.

ARMHOLE BANDS
With 3.25 mm (No. 10) needles and A, evenly pick up and knit 153 sts along armhole edge. Work in rib as for lower band for 3 cm (1¼ in). Cast/bind off in rib.

FRONT BAND
With 3.25 mm (No. 10) needles and A, cast on 13 sts. Work in rib as for lower band for 4 rows.
***5th row:** Rib 5 sts, cast/bind off 3 sts, rib to end.
6th row: Rib 5 sts, cast on 3 sts, rib to end. Work 16 rows in rib as before *. Rep last 18 rows from * to * 5 times more, then cont in rib as before without further buttonholes until band, when slightly stretched fits along right front, round neck, then along left front. Cast/bind off in rib.

TO FINISH
Sew up side seams, sew armhole bands tog. Sew front band in place, matching 6th buttonhole position to beg of right front neck shaping. Sew on buttons.

PAX SOCKS

MATERIALS
7 colours, see key.
50 g (2 oz) balls of Paton's 5 ply Pure Wool Bluebell, or equivalent yarn to give stated tension: A 1 ball; B 2 balls; C 1 ball; D 1 ball; E 1 ball; F 1 ball; G 1 ball.
Pair each 4.00 mm (No. 8) and 3.25 mm (No. 10) knitting needles. Set of four 3.25 mm (No. 10) knitting needles. Stitch holder. Hat elastic.

MEASUREMENTS
Length of sole: 23 cm (9 in)
Length from heel to top: 38 cm (15 in)

TENSION/GAUGE
25½ sts and 27 rows to 10 cm (4 in) over st st in fair isle patt, using 4.00 mm (No. 8) needles. Change needle size if necessary to obtain the stated tension/gauge.

TO MAKE A SOCK

Beg at top. With 3.25 mm (No. 10) needles and A, loosely cast on 92 sts. Work in K1, P1 rib for 7 cm (2¾ in), ending with WS row. Change to 4.00 mm (No. 8) needles and st st. Work from graph beg at 80th row, reading graph downward. Work 20 rows in this manner. Cont to work from graph, reading downward as before at same time dec 1 st at each end of next row, then on every foll 6th row until 74 sts rem. Cont on these 74 sts until 78 rows of patt have been worked.
Change to A only and cont as follows:
Next row: Cast/bind off 1 st, (K2 tog, K2, K2 tog, K3) 8 times.
Next row: Cast/bind off 1 st purlwise, purl to end.
Change to set of four 3.25 mm (No. 10) needles and cont on rem 56 sts as follows:
Next row: K14 on 1st needle, with 2nd needle K28 and leave these 28 sts on 2 spare needles for upper side of foot, slip rem 14 sts onto other end of 1st needle. These 28 sts are for heel.
Work 21 rows of st st on heel sts, always slipping the first st purlwise on a purl row and knitwise on a knit row. Place marker at centre of last row for the beg of sole.

TO TURN HEEL

1st row: K17, K2 tog, K1, *turn*.
2nd row: P8, P2 tog, P1, *turn*.
3rd row: K9, K2 tog, K1, *turn*.
4th row: P10, P2 tog, P1, *turn*.
5th row: K11, K2 tog, K1, *turn*.
Cont in this manner until all sts are worked onto one needle. There should be 18 sts rem at this stage for heel, ending on a purl row.
Next row: K9 and slip these 9 sts onto a stitch holder. The last st of these 9 sts will be the end of rnd. With 1st needle K9, the first st of these 9 sts will be the beg of rnd, then with same needle knit up 12 sts on side of heel piece, with 2nd needle K28 from 2 spare needles for upper side of foot, with 3rd needle knit up 12 sts along other side of heel piece, then K9 from stitch holder (70 sts).
Cont in rnds of st st by knitting on every rnd.

SHAPE FOR INSTEP

1st rnd: Knit.
2nd rnd: 1st needle, knit to last 4 sts, K2 tog, K2; 2nd needle K28; 3rd needle K2, sl1, K1, psso, knit to end of needle.
Rep 1st and 2nd rnds until 14 sts rem on 1st and 3rd needles. Cont on rem 56 sts without further dec until sole measures 18 cm (7 in) or length required.

SHAPE TOES

1st rnd: 1st needle, knit to last 3 sts, K2 tog, K1; 2nd needle, K1, sl1, K1, psso, knit to last 3 sts, K2 tog, K1; 3rd needle, K1, sl1, K1, psso, knit to end of needle (4 sts have been dec).
2nd rnd: Knit.
Rep last 2 rnds until 20 sts rem, then work 1 rnd without dec, then K10 of 1st needle, ending at side of toes. Slip 10 sts of 3rd needle onto other end of 1st needle, then graft or sew sts tog.

TO FINISH

Press lightly. Sew in all ends. Neatly join seam. Turn rib band at top in half to inside and loosely stitch down in place, casing elastic if desired. Make the same for other sock.

Pax is Latin for peace. The dove is the symbol of peace. The Yin-Yang is the balance in nature which brings about peace on the planet.

PAX SCARF

MATERIALS

7 colours, see graph.
50 g (2 oz) balls of Paton's 5 ply Pure Wool Bluebell, or equivalent yarn to give stated tension: A 2 balls; B 2 balls; C 2 balls; D 2 balls; E 1 ball; F 2 balls; G 2 balls.
Pair each 4.00 mm (No. 8) and 3.00 mm (No. 11) knitting needles.

MEASUREMENTS

26 cm x 210 cm (10½ in x 82½ in)

TENSION/GAUGE

27 sts and 29 rows to 10 cm (4 in) over st st in fair isle patt, using 4.00 mm (No. 8) needles. Change needle size if necessary to obtain the stated tension/gauge.

TO MAKE SCARF

With 3.00 mm (No. 11) needles and A, cast on 70 sts. Knit 16 rows. Change to 4.00 mm (No. 8) needles and st st. Work as follows:
1st row: K4 A, work 3rd row of graph as marked on next 62 sts, K4 A.
2nd row: K4 A, work 4th row of graph as marked to last 4 sts, K4 A.
Always working K4 A at each end of every row for borders, follow graph until 55th row has been worked, then rep from 3rd to 55th rows inclusive until work measures 207½ cm (81 in) from beg or length req, ending with WS row. Change to 3.00 mm (No. 11) needles and with A only, knit 16 rows. Cast/bind off loosely.

TO FINISH

Press lightly. Sew in all ends.

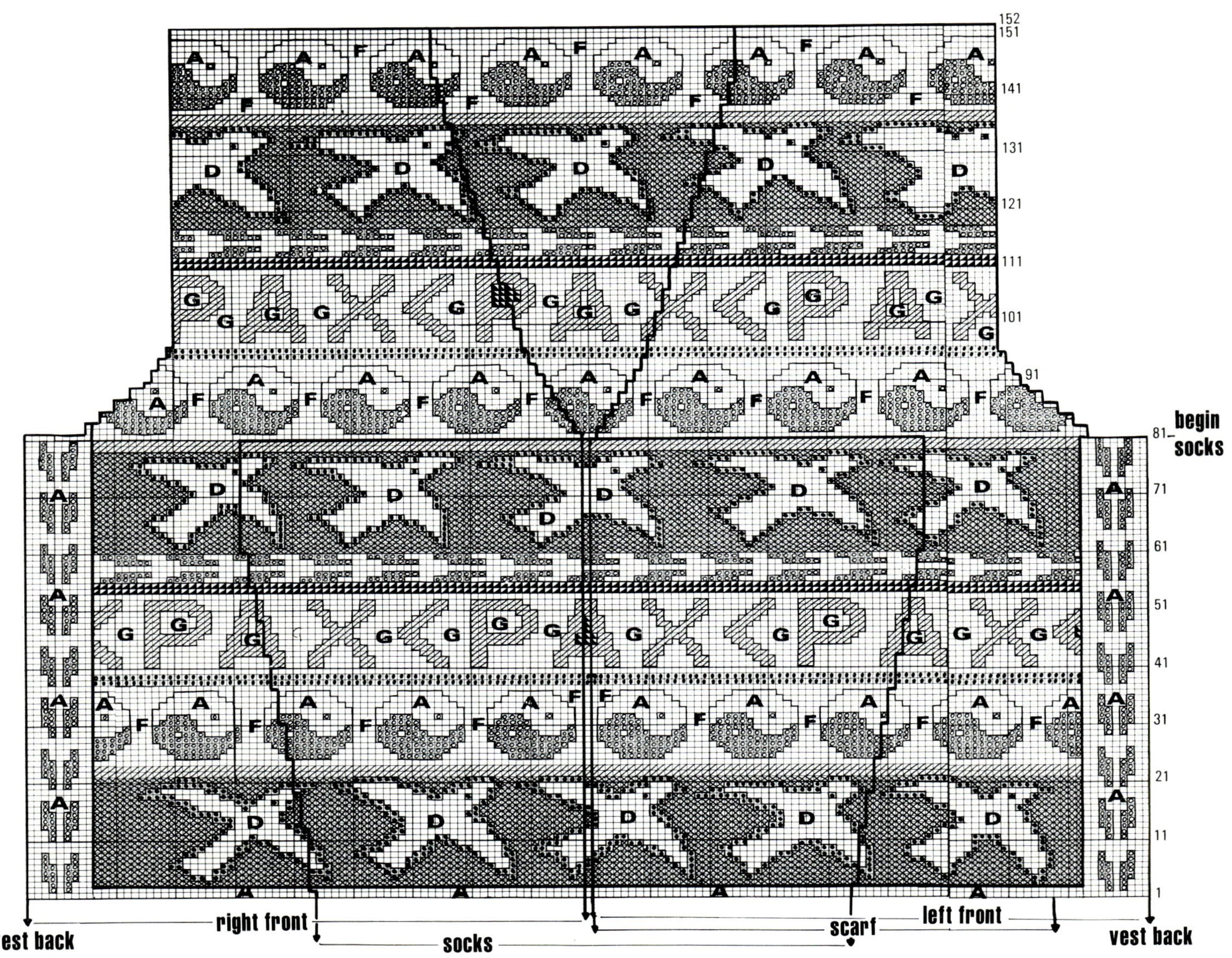

KEY

- A (Black)
- B (Jacaranda Blue)
- C (Pink)
- D (Cream)
- E (Purple)
- F (Aqua)
- G (Red)

BARRAMUNDI

MATERIALS
6 colours, see key.
50 g (2 oz) balls of Paton's 8 ply Pure Wool Herdwick, or equivalent yarn to give stated tension: B 1 ball; C 2 balls; E 7 balls.
50 g (2 oz) balls of Paton's Kid Mohair, or equivalent yarn to give stated tension: A 4 balls; D 2 balls; F 1 ball.
Pair each 4.50 mm (No. 7) and 3.25 mm (No. 10) knitting needles.

MEASUREMENTS (Garment Measures)
Bust: 127 cm (50 in)
Length: 87 cm (34 in)

TENSION/GAUGE
20½ sts and 25 rows to 10 cm (4 in) over st st in picture knit, using 4.50 mm (No. 7) needles. Change needle size if necessary to obtain the stated tension/gauge.

BACK
With 3.25 mm (No. 10) needles and A, cast on 132 sts. Work 11 rows in st st. Knit 1 row for hem line. Change to 4.50 mm (No. 7) needles and cont in st st. Follow graph 1 until 218 rows have been worked.
Next row: Cast/bind off 42 sts for right shoulder, purl until there are 48 sts on right needle, cast/bind off last 42 sts for left shoulder.

CONT FOR NECK FACING
With WS facing, join A to first of 48 sts on needle.

This is inspired by one of the Aboriginal rock paintings at Obiri Rock in Kakadu, home of the Barramundi Dreaming. The Aboriginal rock paintings are open galleries in nature. They are the greatest galleries in the world.

KEY
☐ **A (Black)**
☒ **B (Red)**
⊡ **C (Natural/Cream)**
⊙ **D (Tan)**
▨ **E (Brown)**
◪ **F (Ochre)**
Note: All unlabelled areas to be worked in A as per key.

1st row: Cast on 8 sts for facing extension, then P56 sts.
2nd row: Cast on 8 sts for facing extension, then K64 sts.
Beg with purl row, cont in st st for further 9 rows. Cast/bind off loosely.

FRONT
Work as for back but following graph 2.

TO MAKE UP
Sew in all ends securely. Sew up shoulder seams. Place marker on each side of back and front piece at 23 cm (9 in) below shoulder seams.

ARMHOLE BANDS
Both the same.
With 3.25 mm (No. 10) needles and A, pick up and knit 41 sts on each of back and front pieces (87 sts). Work 9 rows in st st. Purl 1 row. Work 9 rows more in st st. Cast/bind off.

TO FINISH
Sew up side seams and armhole bands taking care to match up continuous Barramundi motif along right hand seam, then fold bands in half to inside and stitch down in place. Fold hem to inside and stitch in place. Fold neck facing to inside at purl row and stitch in place, then stitch extensions to shoulder seam.

back

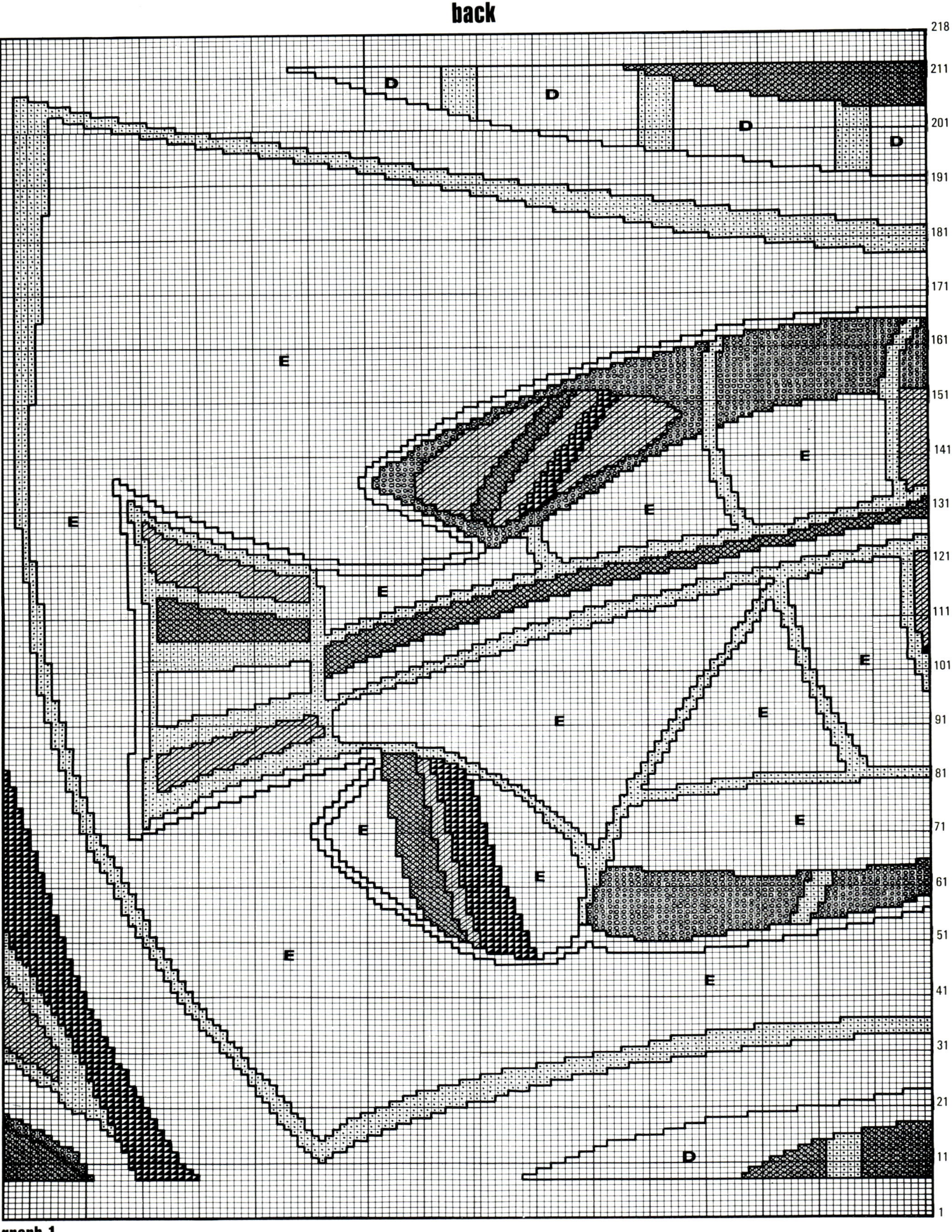
218
211
201
191
181
171
161
151
141
131
121
111
101
91
81
71
61
51
41
31
21
11
1
D
D
D
D
E
E
E
E
E
E
E
E
E
E
E
E
D

graph 1

front

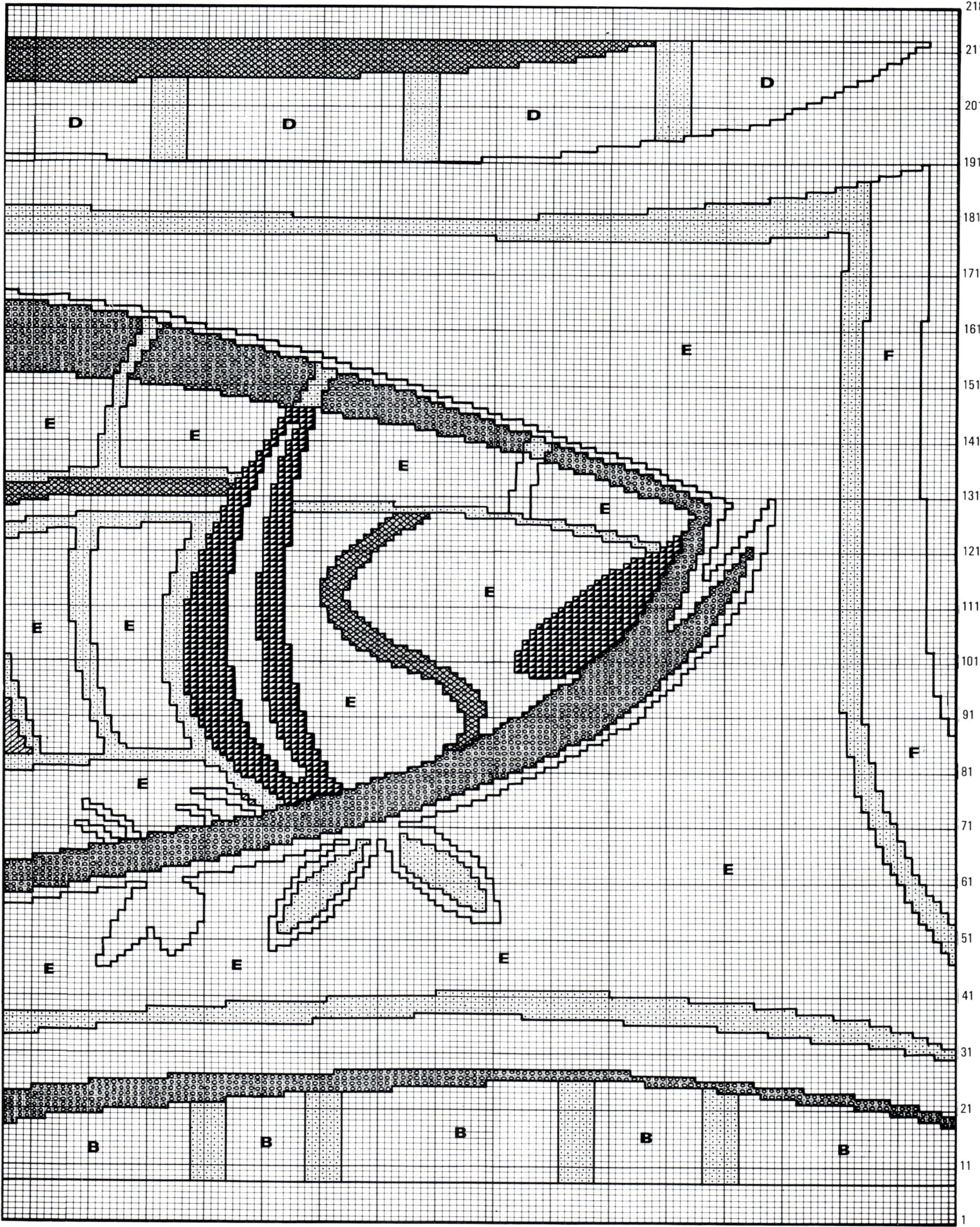

graph 2

MATERIALS

4 colours, see key.
50 g (2 oz) balls of Cleckheaton 8 ply Pure Wool Machine Wash, or equivalent yarn to give stated tension: A 14 balls; B 1 ball; C 2 balls; D 1 ball.
Pair each 4.00 mm (No. 8) and 3.25 mm (No. 10) knitting needles. Set of four 3.25 mm (No. 10) needles. Pair 4.50 mm (No. 7) knitting needles for geometric patt in fair isle knit section.

MEASUREMENTS
(Garment Measures)

Bust: 102 cm (40 in)
Length: 51 cm (20 in)
Sleeve seam: 49 cm (19¼ in)

TENSION/GAUGE

24 sts and 28 rows to 10 cm (4 in) over st st, using 4.00 mm (No. 8) needles. Change needle size if necessary to obtain the stated tension/gauge.

BACK

With 3.25 mm (No. 10) needles and A, cast on 111 sts. Work in K1, P1 rib for 5 cm (2 in), ending with RS row.
Inc row: Rib 11 sts, (inc 1 st in next st, rib 7 sts) rep 12 times in all, rib 4 sts (123 sts).

I love the balance in nature. The red waratah is a symbol of earth and fire. The dolphin is a symbol of the sea and water. The waratah is me in this design and symbolises the love I feel for the dolphins of Monkey Mia.

KEY
☐ **A (White)**
☒ **B (Royal Blue)**
▣ **C (Black)**
◙ **D (Red)**
Note: Use 4.50 mm (No. 7) needles to work in fair isle pattern.

Change to 4.00 mm (No. 8) needles and st st. Work from graph 1 for 56 rows, taking care to use 4.50 mm (No. 7) needles for fair isle pattern.

SHAPE ARMHOLES

Dec 1 st each end of next 7 rows (109 sts rem) *. Cont on these rem sts until 122 rows of graph 1 have been worked.

SHAPE NECK

Next row: Work 39 sts from graph, cast/bind off centre 31 sts loosely, work to end of row. Cont to work on last 39 sts from graph for left side of neck and dec 1 st at neck edge on next 4 rows (35 sts rem). Work 1 row without dec. Cast/bind off.
Ret to rem 39 sts, rejoin yarn at right neck edge. Following graph 1, dec 1 st at neck edge on first 4 rows, then work 1 row without dec. Cast/bind off.

FRONT

Following graph 2, work as for back to * taking care to use 4.50 mm (No. 7) needles for fair isle pattern. Cont on 109 sts until 104 rows of graph 2 have been worked.

SHAPE NECK

Next row: Work 43 sts from graph 2, cast/bind off centre 23 sts loosely, work from graph to end.
Cont on last 43 sts from graph for right side of neck and cast/bind off at neck edge on every alt row 2 sts 2 times, then 1 st 4 times (35 sts rem). Work 11 rows straight from graph. Cast/bind off.
Ret to rem 43 sts, rejoin yarn at left neck edge. Following graph 2, cast/bind off at neck edge on next and every foll alt row 2 sts 2 times, then 1 st 4 times (35 sts rem). Work 12 rows straight from graph. Cast/bind off.

SLEEVES

Both the same.
With 3.25 mm (No. 10) needles and A, cast

graph 2

on 55 sts. Work in K1, P1 rib for 5 cm (2 in), ending with RS row.
Inc row: Rib 5 sts, (inc 1 st in next st, rib 3 sts) rep 12 times in all, rib 2 (67 sts).
Change to 4.00 mm (No. 8) needles and st st. Work from graph 3 at same time inc 1 st each end of 5th row once, then on every foll 6th row 11 times, then on every foll 4th row 10 times, taking care to use 4.50 mm (No. 7) needles for fair isle pattern (111 sts). Work 5 rows straight.

SHAPE TOP

Dec 1 st each end of next 7 rows (97 sts rem). Cast/bind off purlwise.

TO MAKE UP

Press lightly on wrong sides. Sew in all ends securely. Sew shoulder, side and sleeve seams. Set sleeves into armholes and sew evenly.

NECKBAND AND COLLAR

With set of four 3.25 mm (No. 10) needles and C, pick up and knit 25 sts on left side of front neck, 15 sts over centre front and place marker over centre 11 sts of these 15 sts, 25 sts on right side of front neck, 49 sts on back neck (114 sts). *Change to A* and work in rnds of K1, P1 rib for 2.5 cm (1 in).
Next rnd: Rib to the marked 11 sts at centre front neck, cast/bind off these 11 sts in rib, then cont in rib to end.
Rearrange rem 103 sts onto 3 needles. With RS facing, rejoin A to first st after centre 11 sts which are cast/bind off, inc 1 st in 1st st, knit to last st, incl 1 st in last st (105 sts), turn.

CONT FOR COLLAR

1st row: K1, (P1, K1) rep to end, turn.
2nd row: P1, (K1, P1) rep to end, turn.
3rd row: (K1, P1) 8 times, * (K1, yfwd, K1) in back loop of next st, P1, (K1, P1) 8 times, rep from * 3 times more, (K1, yfwd, K1) in back loop of next st, (P1, K1) 8 times (115 sts), turn.
4th, 5th, 6th rows: Work 2nd row, then 1st and 2nd rows once.
7th row: (K1, P1) 15 times, * (K1, yfwd, K1) in back loop of next st, P1, (K1, P1) 8 times, rep from * 3 times more, K1, (P1, K1) 6 times (123 sts).
8th, 9th, 10th rows: Work 2nd row, then 1st and 2nd rows once.
11th row: (K1, P1) 10 times, * (K1, yfwd, K1) in back loop of next st, P1, (K1, P1) 9 times, rep from * 4 times more, K1, P1, K1 (133 sts).
Cont on these 133 sts in rib as before until collar section measures 7.5 cm (3 in). Cast/bind off ribwise loosely.
Turn collar to outside.

back
128
121
111
101
91
81
71
61
51
41
31
21
11
1
graph 1
sleeves
124
121
111
101
91
81
71
61
51
41
31
21
11
1
L·O·V·E·L·O·V·E
graph 3

BANKSIA

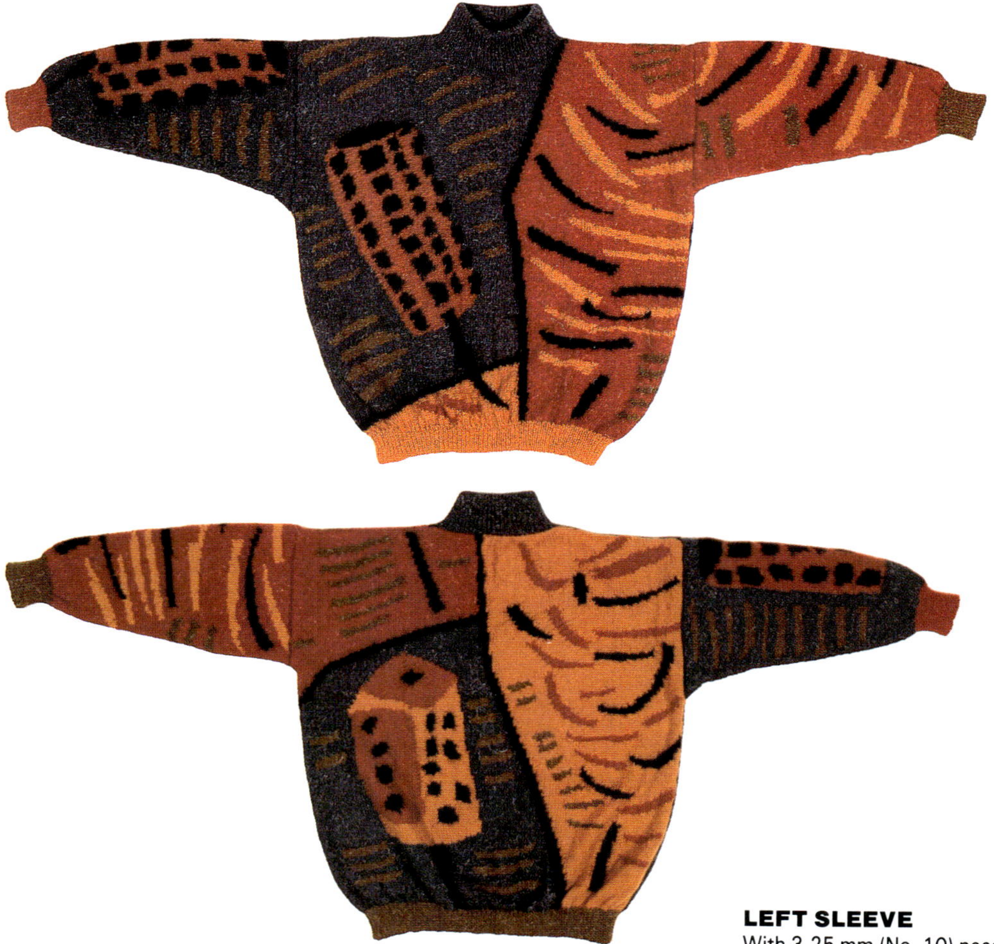

MATERIALS
6 colours, see key.
50 g (2 oz) balls of Paton's 8 ply Pure Wool Herdwick, or equivalent yarn to give stated tension: A 3 balls; D 7 balls; F 5 balls.
50 g (2 oz) balls of Paton's Kid Mohair, or equivalent yarn to give stated tension: B 4 balls; C 2 balls; E 2 balls.
Pair each 4.50 mm (No. 7) and 3.25 mm (No. 10) knitting needles. Set of four 3.25 mm (No. 10) knitting needles.

MEASUREMENTS
(Garment Measures)
Bust: 132 cm (52 in)
Length: 73.5 cm (30 in)
Sleeve seam: 49 cm (19¼ in)

TENSION/GAUGE
21 sts and 26 rows to 10 cm (4 in) over st st in fair isle patt, using 4.50 mm (No. 7) needles. Change needle size if necessary to obtain the stated tension/gauge.

BACK
With 3.25 mm (No. 10) needles and A, cast on 121 sts. Work in K1, P1 rib for 6 cm (2½ in), ending with RS row.
Inc row: (rib 4 sts, inc 1 st in next st) twice, (rib 5 sts, inc 1 st in next st) 16 times, rib 5 sts, (inc 1 st in next st, rib 4 sts) twice (141 sts).
Change to 4.50 mm (No. 7) needles and st st *. Work 182 rows of graph 1. Cast/bind off loosely.

The ancient banksia grows all around me in the Blue Mountains. I love its abstract shape, spiky and tough like the Australian bush, with its ochres, reds and rich oranges, the perfect colours of the earth.

KEY
A (Green)
B (Ochre)
C (Black)
D (Blue)
E (Tan)
F (Red)

FRONT
Work as for back to * using B in place of A. Work 160 rows of graph 2.

SHAPE NECK
Next row: Work 57 sts from graph 2, cast/bind off centre 27 sts, work to end of row. Cont on last 57 sts from graph 2 for right side of neck and cast/bind off at neck edge on every alt row 2 sts 4 times, 1 st 4 times (48 sts rem). Work 5 rows straight from graph. Cast/bind off.
Ret to rem 57 sts, rejoin yarn at left neck edge. Working from graph, cast/bind off at beg of next and every foll alt row 2 sts 4 times, 1 st 4 times. Work 6 rows straight from graph. Cast/bind off.

LEFT SLEEVE
With 3.25 mm (No. 10) needles and A, cast on 55 sts. Work in K1, P1 rib for 6 cm (2½ in), ending with RS row.
Inc row: Rib 6 sts, (inc 1 st in next st, rib 5 sts) 8 times, rib 1 st (63 sts).
Change to 4.50 mm (No. 7) needles and st st **. Working from graph 3, inc 1 st each end of 5th row, then on every foll 4th row until there are 113 sts, then inc 1 st each end of every foll alt row 4 times (121 sts). Work 3 rows straight from graph 3. Cast/bind off loosely.

RIGHT SLEEVE
Using F instead of A work as for left sleeve to **, work from graph 4 shaping sleeve seam as for left sleeve.

TO MAKE UP
Press lightly on wrong sides. Sew in all ends. Sew shoulder seams.

NECKBAND
With rs facing and set of four 3.25 mm (No. 10) needles and D, evenly pick up and knit 73 sts on front neck, 55 sts on back neck (128 sts). Work in rnds of K1, P1 rib for 15 cm (6 in). Cast/bind off ribwise loosely.

TO FINISH
Match centre of sleeve top to shoulder seam and sew sleeves evenly in place, then sew up side and sleeve seams. Fold neckband in half to inside and loosely stitch down in place.

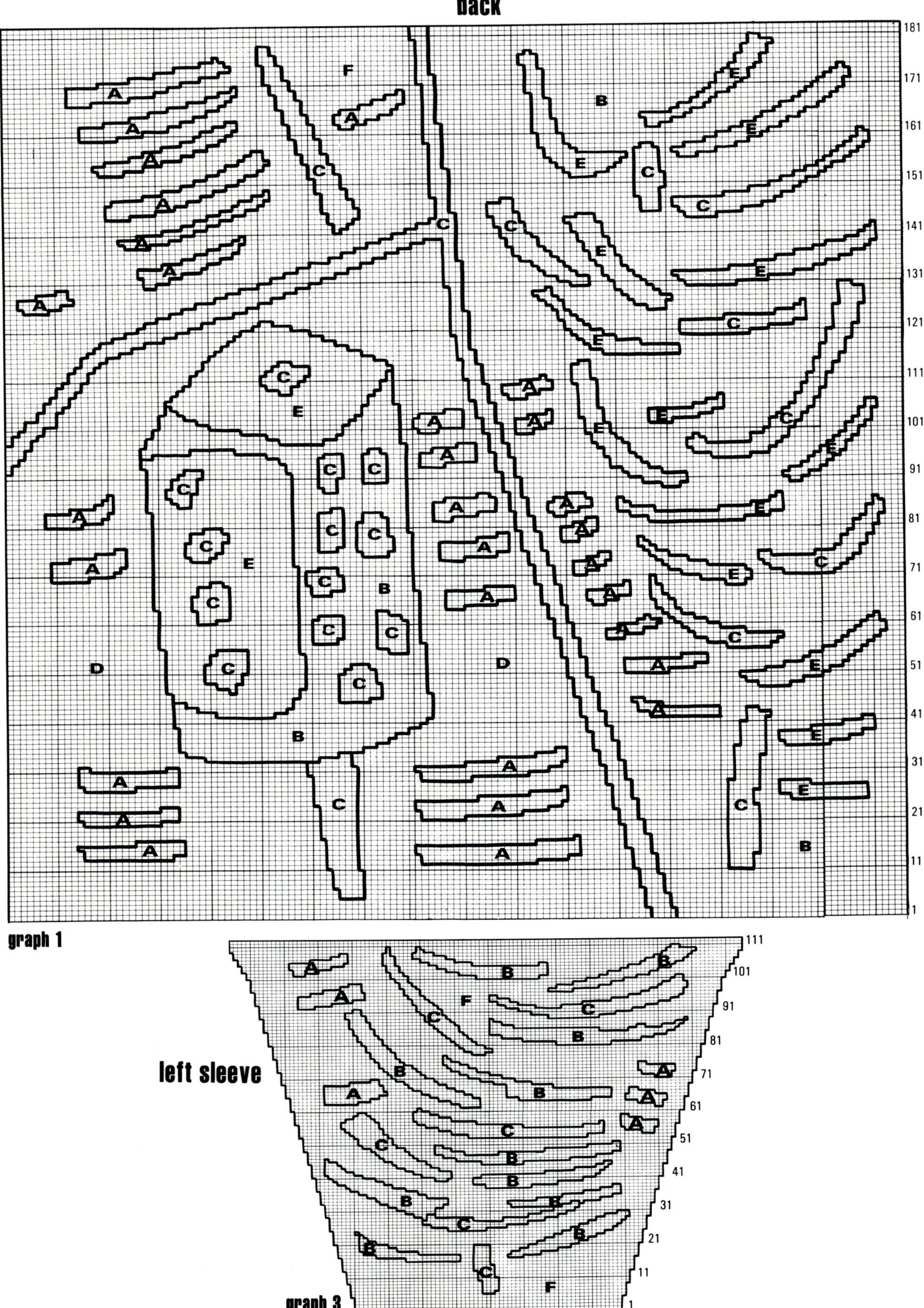
back
graph 1
left sleeve
graph 3

front

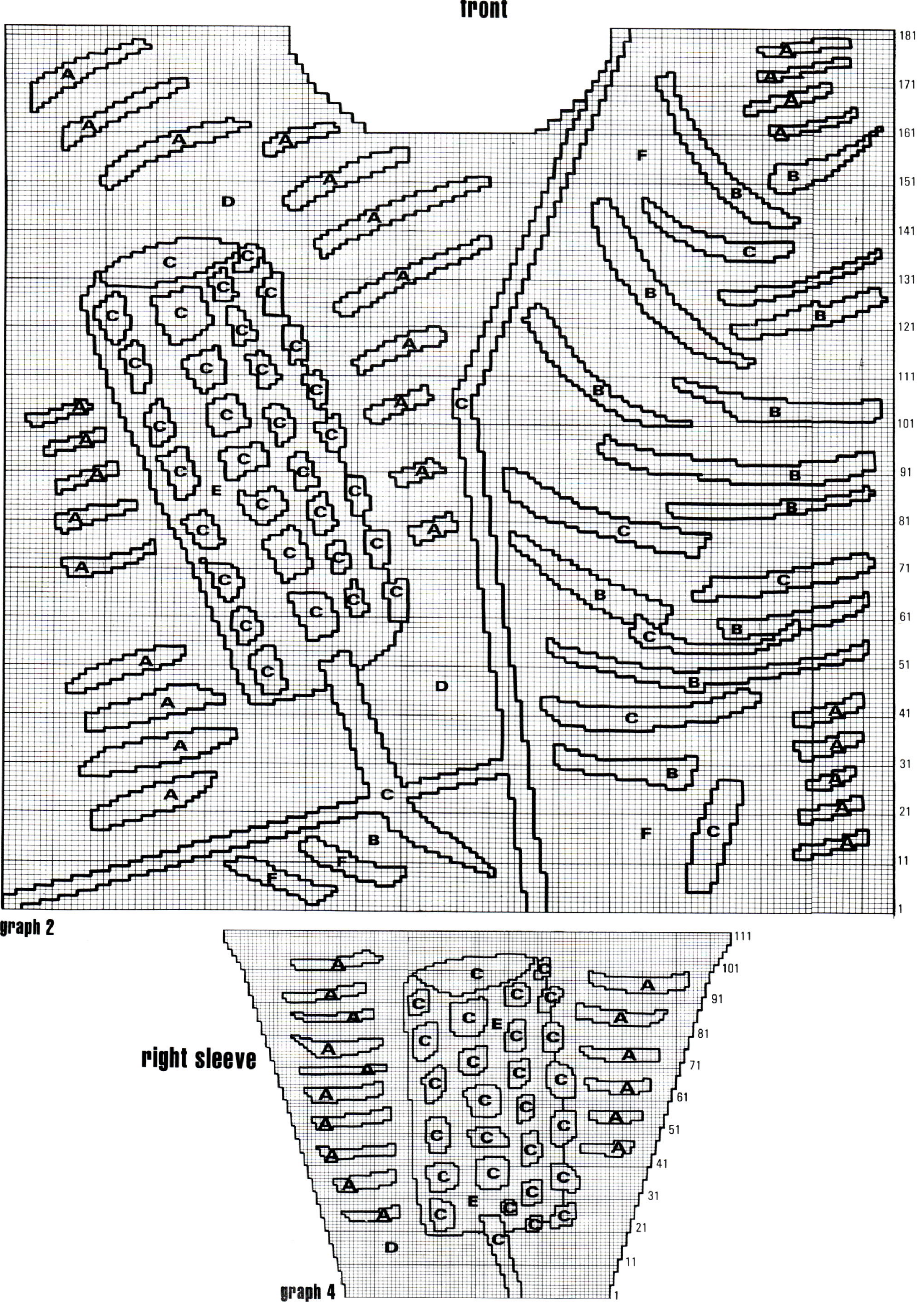

The Aboriginal instrument, the didgeridoo, reminds me that primitive earth sounds inspire primitive earth shapes.

MATERIALS

5 colours, see key.
50 g (2 oz) balls of Paton's 12 ply Pure Wool Jet, or equivalent yarn to give stated tension: A 8 balls; B 5 balls; C 3 balls.
50 g (2 oz) balls of Paton's Woodlands, or equivalent yarn to give stated tension: D 3 balls; E 3 balls.
Pair each 6.00 mm (No. 4) and 5.00 mm (No. 6) knitting needles.

MEASUREMENTS (Garment Measures)

Width across top: 148 cm (58¼ in)
Length: 68.5 cm (27 in)

TENSION/GAUGE

15½ sts and 24 rows to 10 cm (4 in) over st st in picture knit, using 6.00 mm (No. 4) needles. Change needle size if necessary to obtain the stated tension/gauge.

NOTE

When working in moss st, always work 1st row in new colour in st st to keep borders in smooth lines.

SPECIAL ABBREVIATION

Moss st = **1st row:** (K1, P1) rep to end of B and C sections. **2nd row:** Reverse patt sts by working K1 over purl st and P1 over knit st. Rep these 2 rows.

BACK

With 5.00 mm (No. 6) needles and A, cast on 70 sts. Work in K1, P1 rib for 6 rows.
Next row: With A K1, P1, * with B (K1, P1) 5 times, with A (K1, P1) twice, rep from * 3 times more, with B (K1, P1) 5 times, with A K1, P1.
Rep last row until work measures 18 cm (7 in) from beg, ending with RS row. Cont working in these colours, increase as follows:
Inc row: Rib 6 sts, (inc 1 st in next st, rib 2 sts) 20 times, rib 4 sts (90 sts).
Change to 6.00 mm (No. 4) needles and work 120 rows of graph at same time shape Dolman sleeves as follows: inc 1 st each end of 3rd row once, then on every foll 2nd row 39 times more (170 sts). Work 1 row.
Place marker at each end of last row for beg of sleeve edges. Work 38 rows straight as on graph. Cast/bind off loosely.

FRONT

Work as for back until 100 rows of graph have been worked.

SHAPE NECK

Next row: Work 77 sts from graph, cast/bind off centre 16 sts loosely, work from graph to end of row.
Cont on last 77 sts from graph for right side of neck. Dec 1 st at neck edge on every row 7 times, then on every foll alt row 4 times (66 sts rem). Work 4 rows straight from graph. Cast/bind off loosely.
Ret to rem 77 sts, rejoin yarn at left neck edge. Work from graph for left front and dec 1 st at neck edge on every row 7 times, then on every foll alt row 4 times. Work 4 rows straight from graph. Cast/bind off loosely.

TO MAKE UP

Press lightly on wrong sides. Sew in all ends. Sew right shoulder seam.

NECKBAND

With 5.00 mm (No. 6) needles and A, pick up and knit 48 sts on front neck, 36 sts on back neck (84 sts). Work in K1, P1 rib for 5 rows.
Next row: With A K1, * with A (K1, P1) twice, with B (K1, P1) 5 times, rep from * to last st, with B K1.
Next row: With B K1, * with B (K1, P1) 5 times, with A (K1, P1) twice, rep from * to last st, with A K1.
Rep last 2 rows twice, then with A only work 23 rows in rib as before. Cast/bind off ribwise loosely.

CUFFS

Sew left shoulder seam and side of neckband. With 5.00 mm (No. 6) needles and A, pick up and knit 73 sts along sleeve edge. Knit 1 row, Cont as follows:
1st row: With A K1, (P1, K1) twice, with B P1, (K1, P1) 13 times, with A K1, (P1, K1) 4 times, with B P1, (K1, P1) 13 times, with A K1, (P1, K1) twice.
2nd row: With A P1, (K1, P1) twice, with B K1, (P1, K1) 13 times, with A P1, (K1, P1) 4 times, with B K1, (P1, K1) 13 times, with A P1, (K1, P1) twice.
3rd row: With A (K1, P1) twice, sl1, K1, psso, with B (K1, P1) 12 times, K1, with A K2 tog, (P1, K1) 3 times, P1, sl1, K1, psso, with B (K1, P1) 12 times, K1, with A K2 tog, (P1, K1) twice, 4 sts have been decreased.
4th row: With A P1, (K1, P1) twice, with B P1, (K1, P1) 12 times, with A P1, (K1, P1) 4 times, with B P1, (K1, P1) 12 times, with A P1, (K1, P1) twice.
Cont in rib and work 5 sts at each end and 9 sts at centre in A, and all other sts between A sections in B for block patt. Work 2 rows more in block patt, then * work 4 rows in A only in rib, then 6 rows in block patt in rib *, rep from * to * at same time dec 4 sts on 7th, 11th, 15th, 19th, 23rd and 27th rows (45 sts rem), then work 1 row more in block patt.
Cont in A only as follows:
Dec row: K4, (K2 tog, K3) 8 times, K1, (37 sts rem).
Knit 1 row, then cont in K1, P1 rib for further 7.6 cm (3 in). Cast/bind off ribwise. Work the same for other side.

TO FINISH

Sew up side and sleeve seams. Fold neckband in half to inside and loosely stitch down in place.

front and back

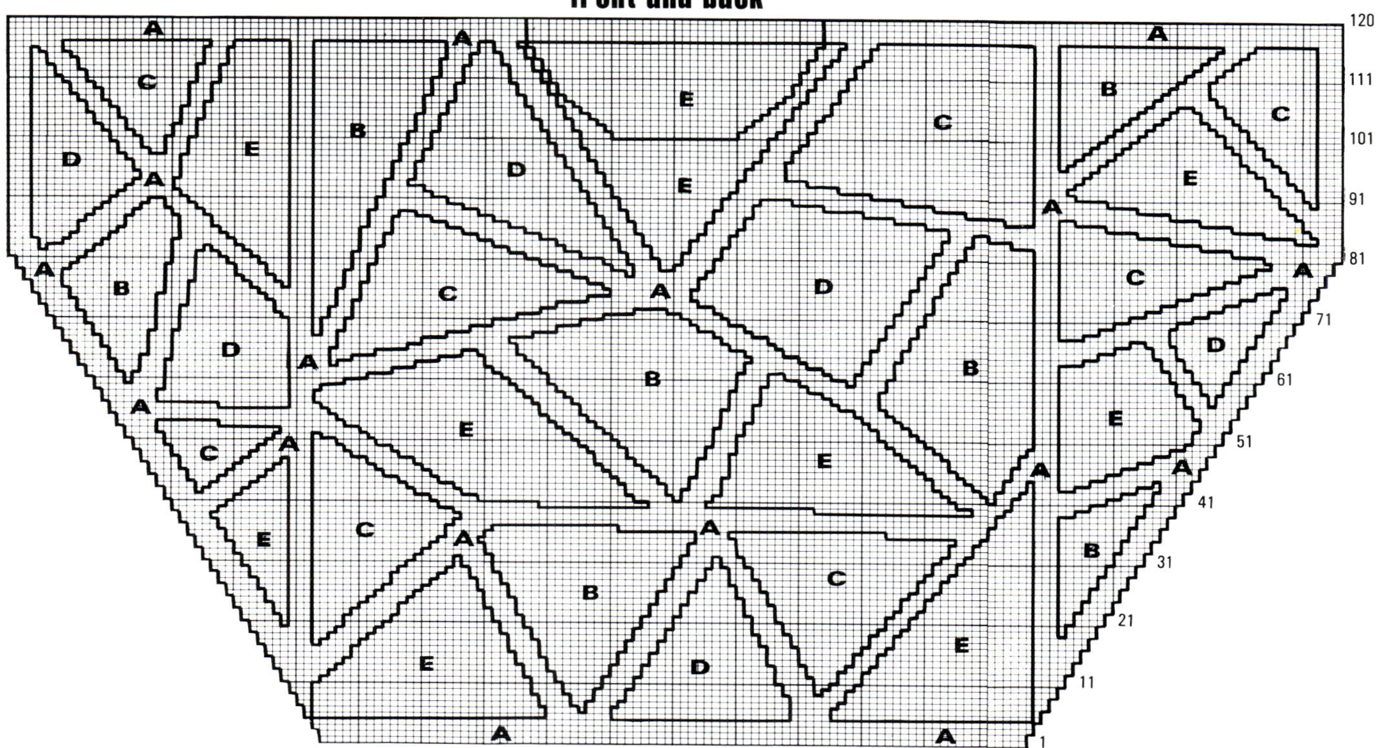

KEY
A Stocking stitch (Black)
B Moss stitch (Grey)
C Moss stitch (Green)
D (Fleck 1)
E (Fleck 2)

MATERIALS

6 colours, see key.
50 g (2 oz) balls of Cleckheaton 8 ply Highland, or equivalent yarn to give stated tension: A 10 balls; C 3 balls; F 2 balls.
50 g (2 oz) balls of Cleckheaton 8 ply Natural, or equivalent yarn to give stated tension: B 2 balls; D 3 balls; E 2 balls.
Pair each 4.50 mm (No. 7) and 3.25 mm (No. 10) knitting needles. Set of four 3.25 mm (No. 10) knitting needles. 4.00 mm (No. 8) crochet hook.

MEASUREMENTS (Garment Measures)

Bust: 127 cm (50 in)
Length: 73 cm (29 in)
Sleeve seam: 47 cm (18½ in)

TENSION/GAUGE

20½ sts and 27 rows to 10 cm (4 in) over st st in picture knit, using 4.50 mm (No. 7) needles. Change needle size if necessary to obtain the stated tension/gauge.

BACK

With 3.25 mm (No. 10) needles and A, cast on 111 sts. Work in K1, P1 rib for 6 cm (2½ in), ending with RS row.
Inc row: Rib 3 sts, (inc 1 st in next st, rib 4 sts) 22 times ending with rib 2 sts instead of rib 4 sts (133 sts).
Change to 4.50 mm (No. 7) needles and st st. Work 182 rows from graph 1. Cast/bind off loosely.

FRONT

Work as for back until 156 rows of graph 1 have been worked.

SHAPE NECK

Next row: Work 57 sts from graph, cast/bind off centre 19 sts loosely, work to end.
Cont on last 57 sts from graph 1 for right side of neck and dec 1 st at neck edge on every row 5 times, then on every alt row 7 times. On 45 sts work 6 rows straight from graph. Cast/bind off loosely.
Ret to rem 57 sts, rejoin yarn at left neck edge. Following graph, dec 1 st at neck edge on every row 5 times, then on every alt row 7 times. On 45 sts work 6 rows straight from graph. Cast/bind off loosely.

SLEEVES

Both the same.
With 3.25 mm (No. 10) needles and A, cast on 53 sts. Work in K1, P1 rib for 6 cm (2½ in), ending with RS row.
Inc row: Rib 3 sts, (inc 1 st in next st, rib 2 sts) 16 times, rib 2 sts (69 sts).
Change to 4.50 mm (No. 7) needles and st st. Working from graph 2, inc 1 st each end of 9th row once, then on every foll 6th row 10 times, then on every foll 4th row 10 times (111 sts). Work 3 rows straight. Cast/bind off loosely.

TO MAKE UP

Press lightly on wrong sides. Sew in all ends. Sew shoulder seams.

NECKBAND

With rs facing and set of four 3.25 mm (No. 10) needles and A, pick up and knit 69 sts on front neck, 47 sts on back neck (116 sts). Work in rnds of K1, P1 rib for 10 cm (4 in). Cast/bind off ribwise loosely.

TO FINISH

Match centre of sleeve top to shoulder seam and sew sleeves in place. Sew up side and sleeve seams. Fold neckband in half to inside and loosely stitch down in place.

SQUIGGLES

With B and crochet hook, join yarn to ends of dotted lines as shown on graph.
Work 4 chains, then attach to garment with a sl st, repeat to complete dotted line.
Squiggles may also be embroidered on in chain stitch.

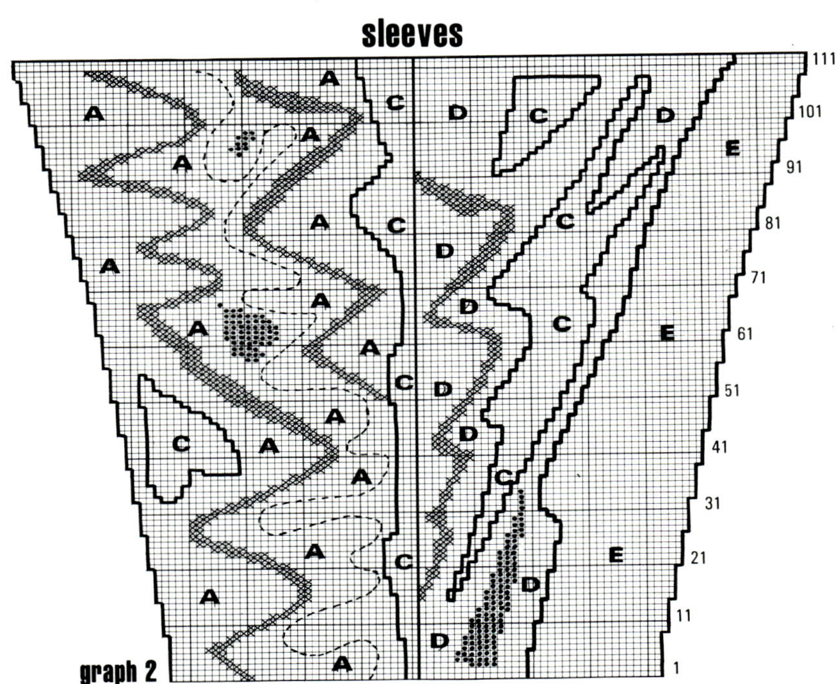

front and back

graph 1

In the bush, the gumleaf falling from the eucalyptus tree is uniquely Australian. The scribbly writings on the trunk of this sacred tree tell secret stories.

KEY
A (Grey)
☒ B (Black)
⊡ C (Red)
D (Brown)
E (Blue)
F (Green)
– – – – squiggle worked by crochet or embroidered chain stitch

MATERIALS
8 colours, see key.
50 g (2 oz) balls of Milford 6 ply Soft Cotton, or equivalent yarn to give stated tension: A 3 balls; B 5 balls; C 2 balls; D 1 ball; E 1 ball; F 1 ball; G 1 ball; H 1 ball.
Pair each 4.50 mm (No. 7) and 3.75 mm (No. 9) knitting needles.

MEASUREMENTS (Garment Measures)
Bust: 117 cm (46 in)
Length: 73 cm (29 in)

TENSION/GAUGE
21 sts and 27 rows to 10 cm (4 in) over st st in picture knit, using 4.50 mm (No. 7) needles. Change needle size if necessary to obtain the stated tension/gauge.

BACK AND FRONT ALIKE
With 3.75 mm (No. 9) needles and A, cast on 125 sts. Work 9 rows in st st. Knit 1 row for hem line. Change to 4.50 mm (No. 7) needles. Work 10 rows from graph.
Next row: Cast on 8 sts for facing extension for side split, work from graph to end. Cast on 8 sts at beg of foll row, and knit to end (141 sts).
Cont until 40 rows of graph have been worked, keeping to graph cast/bind off 8 sts at beg of next 2 rows (125 sts rem). Cont working on rem 125 sts from graph until 198 rows have been worked.

The design of the football fish on top of the star fish symbolises the many different creatures all living together in a very delicate ecological balance.

KEY
A (Pink)
B (Emerald)
▣ **C (Black)**
◙ **D (Purple)**
◪ **E (Yellow)**
F (Light Blue)
G (Red)
H (White)

SHAPE NECK
Next row: With B, cast/bind off 40 sts, then purl next 45 sts on right needle, then cast/bind off last 40 sts.

CONT FOR NECK FACING AS FOLLOWS
With WS facing, rejoin B to 1st of centre 45 sts.
1st row: Cast on 8 sts for facing extension, P53.
2nd row: Cast on 8 sts for facing extension, K61.
Cont in st st on these 61 sts for further 9 rows. Cast/bind off loosely.

TO MAKE UP
Press lightly on wrong sides. Sew in all ends securely. Sew shoulder seams over 40 sts. Fold neck facing at purl row to inside and neatly stitch down in place, then stitch down facing extensions loosely. Place marker on each side edge of back and front at 20 cm (8 in) below shoulders to denote armhole positions.

ARMHOLE BANDS
Both the same. With 3.75 mm (No. 9) needles and A, pick up and knit 38 sts on each of back and front piece between markers (76 sts). Work in K1, P1 rib for 3 cm (1¼ in). Cast/bind off ribwise. Sew up side seams above side splits and armhole bands. Fold hems and facing for side splits to inside and stitch down in place.

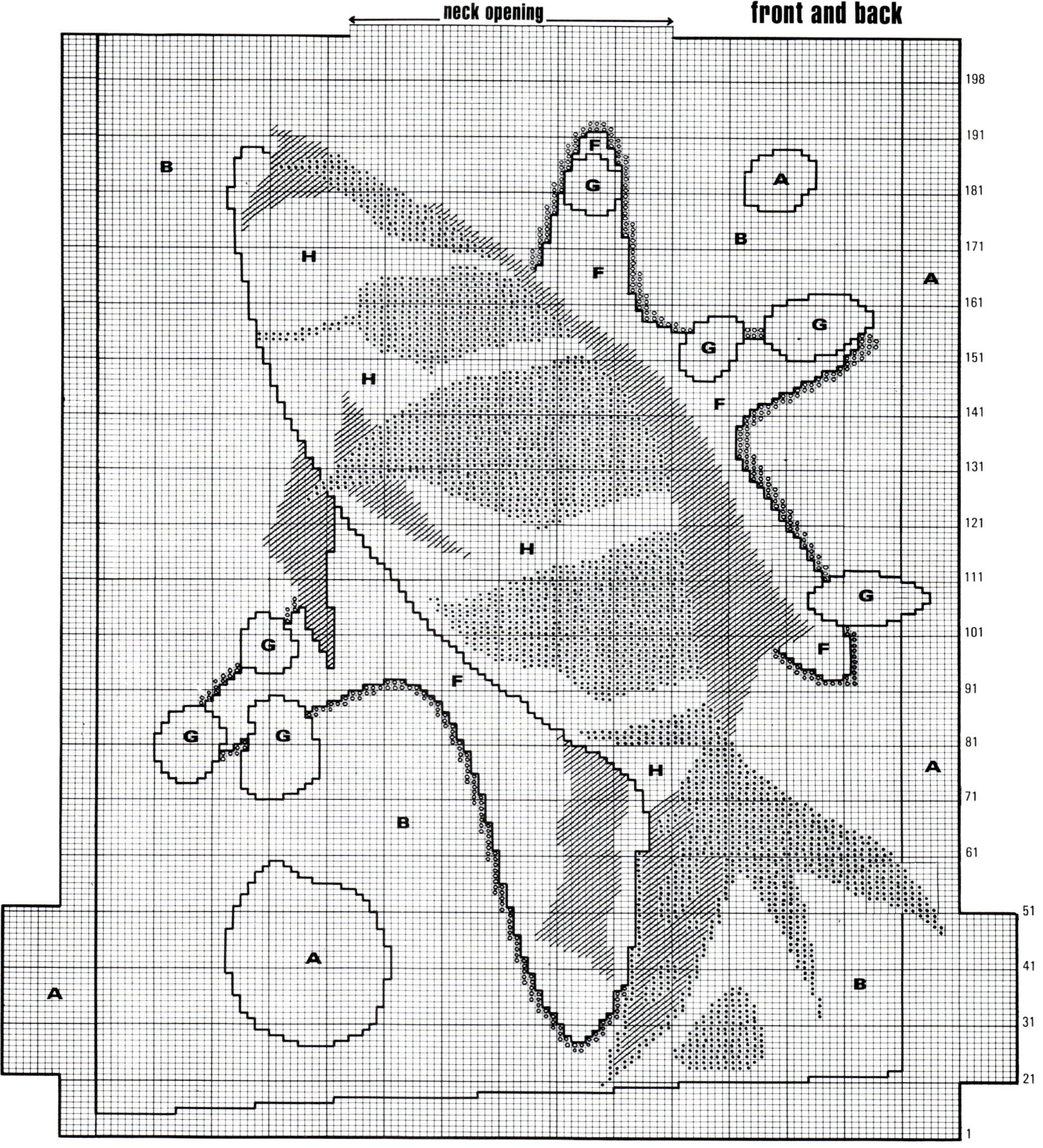
neck opening
front and back
198
191
181
171
161
151
141
131
121
111
101
91
81
71
61
51
41
31
21
1
A
B
F
G
H

BARRIER REEF JUMPER

MATERIALS
10 colours, see key.
50 g (2 oz) balls of Milford 6 ply Soft Cotton, or equivalent yarn to give stated tension: A 3 balls; B 2 balls; C 3 balls; D 3 balls; E 5 balls; F 1 ball; G 2 balls; H 2 balls; I 1 ball; J 1 ball.
Pair each 4.00 mm (No. 8) and 3.00 mm (No. 11) knitting needles. Set of four 3.00 mm (No. 11) knitting needles.

MEASUREMENTS (Garment Measures)
Bust: 117 cm (46 in)
Length: 71 cm (28 in)
Sleeve seam: 44 cm (17¼ in)

TENSION/GAUGE
25 sts and 29 rows to 10 cm (4 in) over st st in fair isle patt, using 4.00 mm (No. 8) needles. Change needle size if necessary to obtain the stated tension/gauge.

BACK
With 3.00 mm (No. 11) needles and E, cast on 146 sts. Work in K1, P1 rib for 6 cm (2½ in), ending with WS row. Change to 4.00 mm (No. 8) needles and st st. Work from graph for jumper until 160 rows have been worked.

SHAPE NECK

Next row: Work 50 sts from graph, cast/bind off centre 46 sts, work to end of row.
Cont on last 50 sts. Cast/bind off 2 sts at left neck edge on every alt row 3 times (44 sts rem). Work 4 rows straight. Cast/bind off, using G only.
Ret to rem 50 sts, rejoin yarn at right neck edge and work from graph, at same time cast off 2 sts at neck edge on next and every foll alt row 3 times (44 sts rem). Work 4 rows straight. Cast/bind off, using G only.

FRONT
Work as for back until 148 rows of graph for jumper have been worked.

SHAPE NECK

Next row: Work 63 sts from graph, cast/bind off centre 20 sts, work to end of row.
Cont on last 63 sts for right side of neck, working from the graph for jumper and cast/bind off at neck edge on every alt row 4 sts 3 times, 2 sts 3 times, 1 st once (44 sts rem). Work 8 rows straight. Cast/bind off, using G only. Ret to rem 63 sts, rejoin yarn at left neck edge and work from the graph at same time cast/bind off at neck edge at beg of next and every foll alt row 4 sts 3 times, 2 sts 3 times, 1 st once (44 sts rem). Work 8 rows straight from graph. Cast/bind off, using G only.

SLEEVES
With 3.00 mm (No. 11) needles and E, cast on 82 sts. Work in K1, P1 rib for 7 cm (2¾ in), ending with WS row. Change to 4.00 mm (No. 8) needles and st st. Working from graph for sleeve inc 1 st at each end of every 4th row until there are 132 sts. Cont straight until 104 rows of graph for sleeve have been worked. Cast/bind off.

TO MAKE UP
Press lightly on wrong sides. Sew in all ends securely. Sew shoulder seams. Matching centre of sleeve top to shoulder seam, sew sleeves in place, then sew up side and sleeve seams.

NECKBAND
With set of four 3.00 mm (No. 11) needles and E, pick up and knit 78 sts on front neck, 64 sts on back neck (142 sts). Work in rnds of K1, P1 rib for 6 cm (2½ in). Cast/bind off ribwise loosely. Fold band in half to inside and stitch down in place.

BARRIER REEF TOP

MATERIALS

10 colours, see key.
50 g (2 oz) balls of Milford 6 ply Soft Cotton, or equivalent yarn to give stated tension: A 1 ball; B 1 ball; C 1 ball; D 1 ball; E 4 balls; F 1 ball; G 1 ball; H 1 ball; I 1 ball; J 1 ball.
Pair each 4.50 mm (No. 7) 3.00 mm (No. 11) knitting needles. Set of four 3.00 mm (No. 11) knitting needles.

MEASUREMENTS (Garment Measures)

Bust: 109 cm (43 in)
Length: 47 cm (18½ in)

TENSION/GAUGE

24 sts and 26 rows to 10 cm (4 in) over st st in fair isle patt, using 4.50 mm (No. 7) needles. Change needle size if necessary to obtain the stated tension/gauge.

BACK

With 3.00 mm (No. 11) needles and E, cast on 123 sts. Work in K1, P1 rib for 6 cm (2½ in), ending on RS row.
Inc row: Rib 11 sts, * inc 1 st in next st, rib 9 sts, rep from * 10 times more, ending with rib 11 sts instead of rib 9 sts (134 sts).
Change to 4.50 mm (No. 7) needles and st st. Work from graph for top until 98 rows of the graph have been worked.

SHAPE NECK AND SHOULDERS

Next row: Work 43 sts from graph, cast/bind off centre 48 sts, work to end of row.
** Cont on last 43 sts, shape left shoulder by casting/binding off at beg of next and each alt row 10 sts 3 times, 9 sts once, at same time shape neck by decreasing 1 st at neck edge on first 4 rows.
Ret to rem 43 sts, rejoin yarn at right neck edge and work 1 row, then shape as other side from **.

FRONT

Work as for back until 64 rows of graph for little top have been worked.

SHAPE NECK

Next row: Work 67 sts from graph, *turn*.
Cont on these 67 sts for left side of neck from graph * and dec 1 st at neck edge on *every row* 18 times. Work 1 row without dec, then dec 1 st at neck edge on next 2 rows. Rep last 3 rows 4 times more, ending with WS row (39 sts rem).
Shape shoulder: Cast/bind off at beg of next and each alt row 10 sts 3 times, then 9 sts once.
Ret to rem 67 sts, rejoin yarn at neck edge and work for left side of neck from graph until 39 sts rem, ending with WS row. Work 1 row without dec, then shape shoulder as for left side.

TO MAKE UP

Press lightly on wrong sides. Sew in all ends. Sew shoulder seams, then sew up side seams, leaving 19 cm (7½ in) from shoulder for armholes.

NECKBAND

With set of four 3.00 mm (No. 11) needles and E, pick up and knit 40 sts on left side of front neck, K1 at V point and place marker in this st, pick up and knit 40 sts on right side of front neck, 61 sts on back neck (142 sts).
1st rnd: (K1, P1) 19 times, K1, * slip next 2 sts tog, K1, pass the 2 sl sts tog over the st just knitted — 2 sts have been dec *after* the st at V point *, (K1, P1) rep to end.
2nd rnd: Knit all knit sts and purl all purl sts as on needle.
3rd rnd: Rib as on needle to 1 st *before* the st at V point, rep from * to * of 1st rnd, cont in rib to end.
Rep last 2 rnds twice, then 2nd rnd once more. Cast/bind off ribwise.

ARMHOLE BANDS

With set of four 3.00 mm (No. 11) needles and E, pick up and knit 45 sts on each of back and front piece (90 sts). Work 8 rnds in K1, P1 rib. Cast/bind off ribwise.

My first time snorkelling in the reef was a life-changing revelation of colour. My imagination ran wild with the patterns in the water and the exotic nature of the fish and plant life.

BARRIER REEF SKIRT

MATERIALS

10 colours, see key.
50 g (2 oz) balls of Milford 4 ply Soft Cotton, or equivalent yarn to give stated tension: A 2 balls; B 1 ball; C 2 balls; D 2 balls; E 2 balls; F 1 ball; G 1 ball; H 1 ball; I 2 balls; J 1 ball.
Pair each 3.75 mm (No. 9), 3.25 mm (No. 10) and 3.00 mm (No. 11) knitting needles.
2.5 cm (1 in) wide elastic for waist.

MEASUREMENTS

Hips: 96.5 cm (38 in)
Length with waistband: 60 cm (23½ in)

TENSION/GAUGE

30 sts and 28 rows to 10 cm (4 in) over st st in fair isle patt, using 3.75 mm (No. 9) needles. Change needle size if necessary to obtain the stated tension/gauge.

BACK AND FRONT ALIKE

With 3.00 mm (No. 11) needles and A, cast on 292 sts. Work 13 rows in st st. Knit 1 row for hem line. Change to 3.75 mm (No. 9) needles and cont in st st, working from graph for jumper twice. On second sequence, work until 116 rows of the graph are complete.
Change to 3.25 mm (No. 10) needles.

SHAPE FOR WAIST

Next row: With A, (K2 tog) rep to end (146 sts rem).
Beg with 118th row, cont to work from the graph until 162 rows have been worked.
Change to 3.00 mm (No. 11) needles and I. Work 13 rows in st st. Knit 1 row, then work 12 rows more in st st. Cast/bind off loosely.

TO MAKE UP

Press lightly on wrong sides. Sew in all ends securely. Sew up side seams. Fold hem to inside and stitch down in place. Cut elastic to fit round waist firmly. Fold waistband at purl row and stitch down, leaving about 5 cm (2 in) open. Thread elastic through waistband, sew ends of elastic together. Stitch down remaining 5 cm (2 in) of waistband.

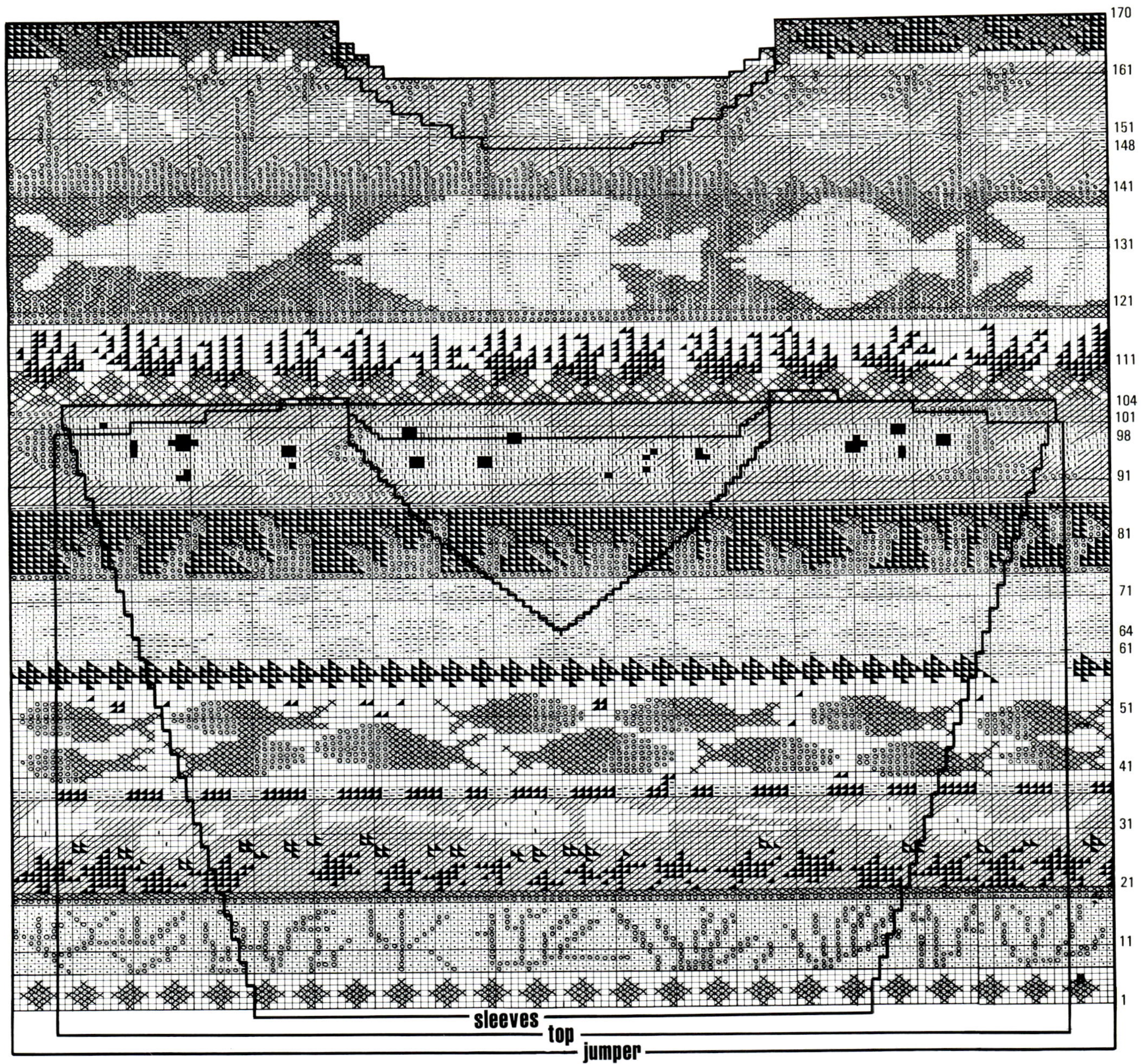

KEY

- ☐ A (Purple)
- ☒ B (Yellow)
- ⊡ C (Aqua)
- ◎ D (Red)
- ◪ E (Light Blue)
- ◢ F (Orange)
- ◣ G (Green)
- ⎅ H (Black)
- ⊟ I (Pink)
- ■ J (White)

DOLPHINS TABARD

MATERIALS
5 colours, see key.
50 g (2 oz) balls of Milford 6 ply Soft Cotton, or equivalent yarn to give stated tension: A 8 balls; B 3 balls; C 3 balls; D 1 ball; E 1 ball. Pair each 4.50 mm (No. 7) and 3.75 mm (No. 9) knitting needles. Set of four 3.25 mm (No. 10) knitting needles.

MEASUREMENTS (Garment Measures)
Bust: 130 cm (51 in)
Length: 91.5 cm (36 in)

TENSION/GAUGE
20 sts and 26 rows to 10 cm (4 in) over st st in picture knit, using 4.50 mm (No. 7) needles. Change needle size if necessary to obtain the stated tension/gauge.

BACK
With 3.75 mm (No. 9) needles and A, cast on 130 sts loosely. Work in st st for 3 cm (1¼ in) ending on a knit row. Knit 1 row for hem line. Change to 4.50 mm (No. 7) needles and cont in st st, following graph 1. Cast/bind off.

FRONT
Work as for back until hem line has been worked. Change to 4.50 mm (No. 7) needles and cont in st st, following graph 2 until 214 rows have been worked.

This is inspired by a fresco from one of the walls of the ancient Palace of Knossos in Crete. The Minoans worshipped the dolphin as a god. They loved and respected the natural world as I do. Let us learn from the past to create a better future.

KEY
A (Royal Blue)
☒ B (Black)
C (White)
D (Turquoise)
E (Orange)

SHAPE NECK
Next row: Work 51 sts from graph 2, cast/bind off centre 28 sts, work to end of row. Cont on last 51 sts from graph 2, cast off at right neck edge on every alt row 2 sts twice, 1 st 4 times (43 sts rem). Work 9 rows straight. Cast/bind off.
Ret to rem 51 sts. Rejoin yarn at left neck edge and cast off at neck edge on next and every foll alt row 2 sts twice, 1 st 4 times (43 sts rem). Work 9 rows straight. Cast/bind off.

TO MAKE UP
Press lightly on wrong sides. Sew in all ends securely. Sew shoulder seams. Sew up side seams, leaving 20 cm (8 in) from shoulder for armholes. Turn up hem, sew in place.

NECKBAND
With RS facing, set of four 3.25 mm (No. 10) needles and A, beg at left shoulder, pick up and knit 20 sts on left side of front neck, 28 sts on centre front neck, 20 sts on right side of front neck, 44 sts on back neck (112 sts).
* Change to C and work in K1, P1 rib for 8 rnds, then with B work 4 rnds. Cast/bind off ribwise loosely.

ARMHOLE BANDS
Both the same.
With RS facing, set of four 3.25 mm (No. 10) needles and A, pick up and knit 45 sts on each of front and back (90 sts). Work as for neckband from *.

front

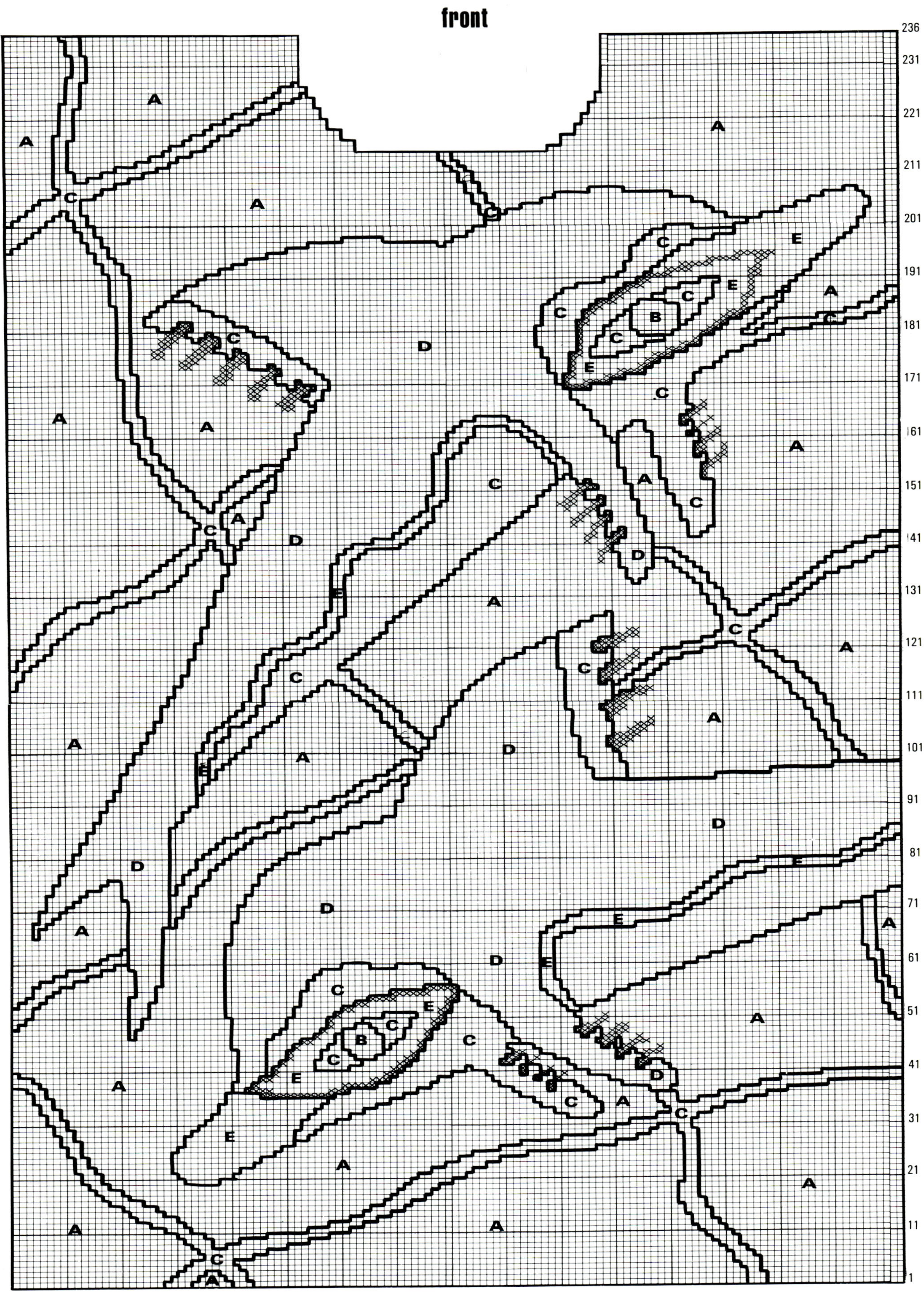

graph 2

back

236
231
221
211
201
191
181
171
161
151
141
131
121
111
101
91
81
71
61
51
41
31
21
11
1
A
B
C
D
E

graph 1

DOLPHINS TOP

MATERIALS
5 colours, see key.
50 g (2 oz) balls of Milford 6 ply Soft Cotton, or equivalent yarn to give stated tension: A 4 balls; B 1 ball; C 3 balls; D 1 ball; E 1 ball.
Pair each 4.50 mm (No. 7) and 3.25 mm (No. 10) knitting needles. Set of four 3.25 mm double pointed (No. 10) knitting needles.

MEASUREMENTS (Garment Measures)
Bust: 104 cm (41 in)
Length: 60 cm (23½ in)

TENSION/GAUGE
21 sts and 26 rows to 10 cm (4 in) over st st in picture knit, using 4.50 mm (No. 7) needles. Change needle size if necessary to obtain the stated tension/gauge.

BACK
With 3.25 mm (No. 10) needles and B, cast on 99 sts. Work in K1, P1 rib for 2 rows. Change to C and cont in rib until 9 cm (3½ in) from beg, ending on RS row.
Inc row: Rib 7 sts, * inc 1 st in next st, rib 4 sts, rep from * 17 times more, ending with rib 6 sts instead of 4 sts (117 sts) **.
Change to 4.50 mm (No. 7) needles and st st. Work 110 rows of graph 1.

SHAPE NECK

Next row: Work 48 sts from graph 1, cast/bind off centre 21 sts, work from graph 1 to end.
Cont on last 48 sts. Cont from graph 1 and cast/bind off at right neck edge on every alt row 2 sts 3 times, 1 st 4 times (38 sts rem). Work 9 rows straight from graph 1. Cast/bind off.
Ret to rem 48 sts. Rejoin yarn at left neck edge and cast/bind off at neck edge on next and every foll alt row 2 sts 3 times, 1 st 4 times (38 sts rem). Work 10 rows straight. Cast/bind off.

Playing with the dolphins at Monkey Mia in Western Australia, I understood the affinity the Minoans had with dolphins. I believe Monkey Mia must be cleared of pollution for the sake of the dolphins.

KEY
A (Royal Blue or Turquoise)
☒ **B (Black)**
C (White)
D (Turquoise or Royal Blue)
E (Orange)

FRONT
Work as back to **. Change to 4.50 mm (No. 7) needles and st st. Work 110 rows from graph 2.

SHAPE NECK

Work and finish as for back neck shaping but following graph 2.

TO MAKE UP
Press lightly on wrong sides. Sew in all ends securely. Sew shoulder seams, then sew up side seams, leaving 19 cm (7½ in) from shoulder for armholes.

NECKBAND
With RS facing, set of four 3.25 mm (No. 10) needles and A, beg at left shoulder, pick up and knit 23 sts on left side of front neck, 21 sts on centre front neck, 23 sts on right side of front neck, 23 sts on right side of back neck, 21 sts on centre back neck, 23 sts on left side of back neck (134 sts).
* Change to C and work 9 rnds of K1, P1 rib. Change to B and work 2 rnds in rib. Cast/bind off ribwise loosely.

ARMHOLE BANDS
Both the same. With RS facing, set of four 3.25 mm (No. 10) needles and A, pick up and knit 44 sts on each of back and front piece (88 sts), then work as for neckband from *.

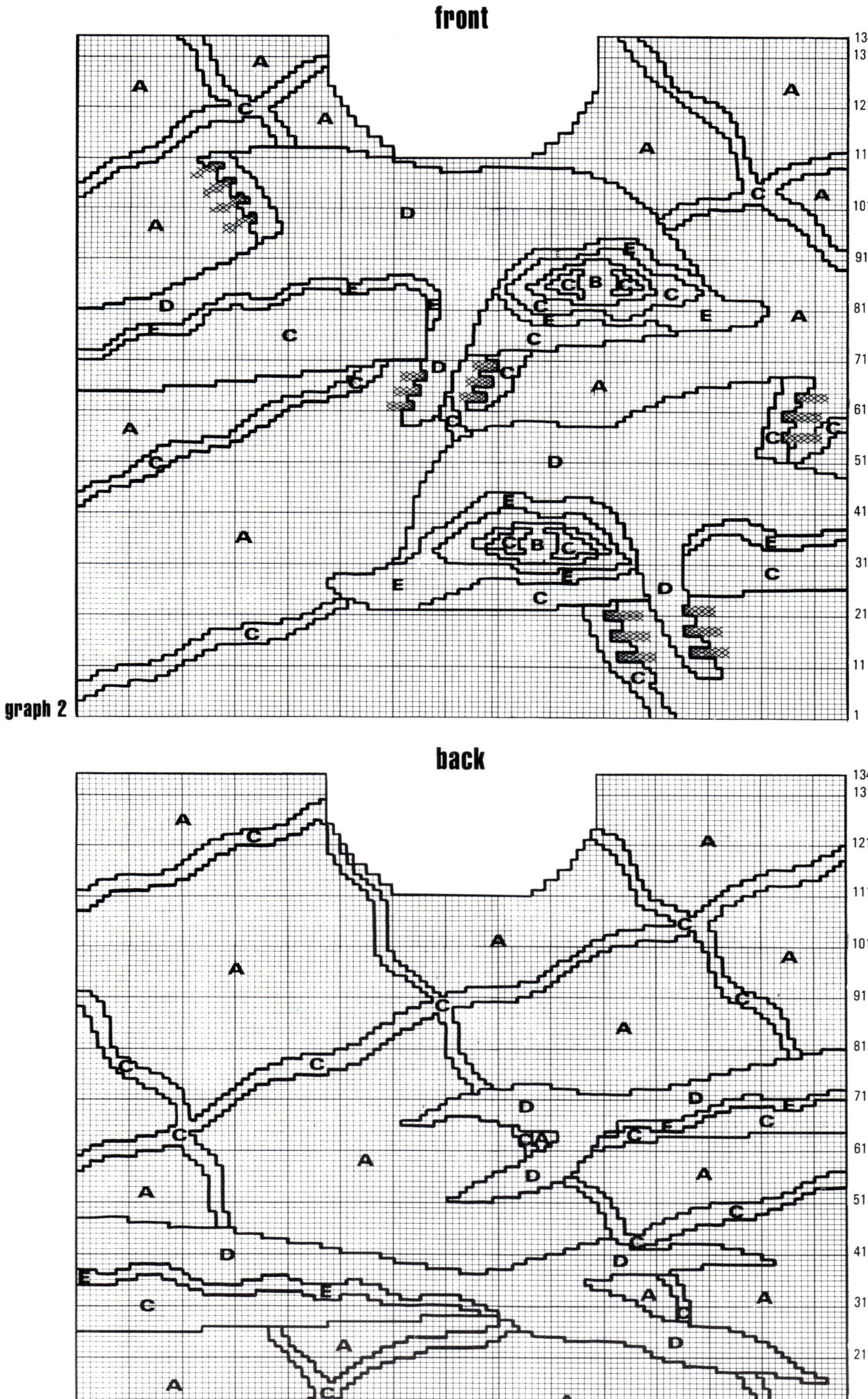
front
graph 2
134
131
121
111
101
91
81
71
61
51
41
31
21
11
1
back
graph 1
134
131
121
111
101
91
81
71
61
51
41
31
21
11
1

MATERIALS
8 colours, see key.
50 g (2 oz) balls of Milford 4 ply Soft Cotton, or equivalent yarn to give stated tension: A 2 balls; B 1 ball; C 1 ball; D 1 ball; E 1 ball; F 2 balls; G 1 ball; H 1 ball.
Pair each 3.25 mm (No. 10) and 2.75 mm (No. 12) knitting needles. Set of four 2.75 mm (No. 12) knitting needles.

MEASUREMENTS (Garment Measures)
Bust: 115 cm (45 in)
Length: 56 cm (22 in)

TENSION/GAUGE
27 sts and 37 rows to 10 cm (4 in) over st st in picture knit, using 3.25 mm (No. 10) needles. Change needle size if necessary to obtain the stated tension/gauge.
Note: Work all spots on Stingray motif in graph A in moss stitch.

BACK
With 2.75 mm (No. 12) needles and A, cast on 138 sts loosely. Work in K1, P1 rib for 9 cm (3½ in), ending on RS row.
Inc row: Rib 9 sts, * inc 1 st in next st, rib 6 sts, rep from * 17 times more ending with rib 9 sts (156 sts) **.
Change to 3.25 mm (No. 10) needles and st st. Work 116 rows from graph 1.

SHAPE SLEEVES
Next row: Cast on 19 sts and work 117th row of graph 1 to end.
Next row: Cast on 19 sts and work 118th row of graph 1 to end.
Cont on these 194 sts from graph 1 until 150 rows have been worked.

SHAPE NECK
Next row: Work 83 sts from graph, cast/bind off centre 28 sts, work from graph to end. Cont on last 83 sts from graph and cast/bind off at neck edge on every foll alt row 2 sts 5 times, 1 st 5 times (68 sts rem). Work 13 rows straight, following graph. Cast/bind off. Ret to rem 83 sts, rejoin yarn at neck edge and cast/bind off at neck edge on next and every foll alt row 2 sts 5 times in all, 1 st 5 times (68 sts rem). Work 14 rows straight, cast/bind off.

What a shock to face one of these creatures! The wealth and diversity of life in the reef is astounding.

KEY
A (Turquoise)
B (Purple)
C (Yellow)
D (Red)
E (Lime Green)
F (Pink)
G (Orange)
H (Emerald)
⍓ Moss stitch (Turquoise)

FRONT
Work as back to **. Change to 3.25 mm (No. 10) needles and st st. Following graph 2, work 116 rows, then shape sleeves and neck as for back. Cast/bind off.

TO MAKE UP
Press lightly on wrong sides. Sew in all ends securely. Sew up right shoulder, side and sleeve seams.

NECKBAND
With RS facing, pair of 2.75 mm (No. 12) needles, beg at left shoulder neck edge and using F, pick up and knit 29 sts on left side of front neck, 28 sts on centre front neck, 29 sts on right side of front neck, 29 sts on right side of back neck, 28 sts on centre back neck, 29 sts on left side of back neck (172 sts). Work in rows of K1, P1 rib for 3.5 cm (1¼ in). Cast/bind off ribwise loosely. Sew left shoulder seam and neckband.

SLEEVE BANDS
With RS facing, set of 2.75 mm (No. 12) needles and H, pick up and knit 60 sts each along back and front of left armhole (120 sts). Work in rnds of K1, P1 rib for 3.5 cm (1¼ in). Cast/bind off ribwise. Work right sleeve band in same way, but using F.

back

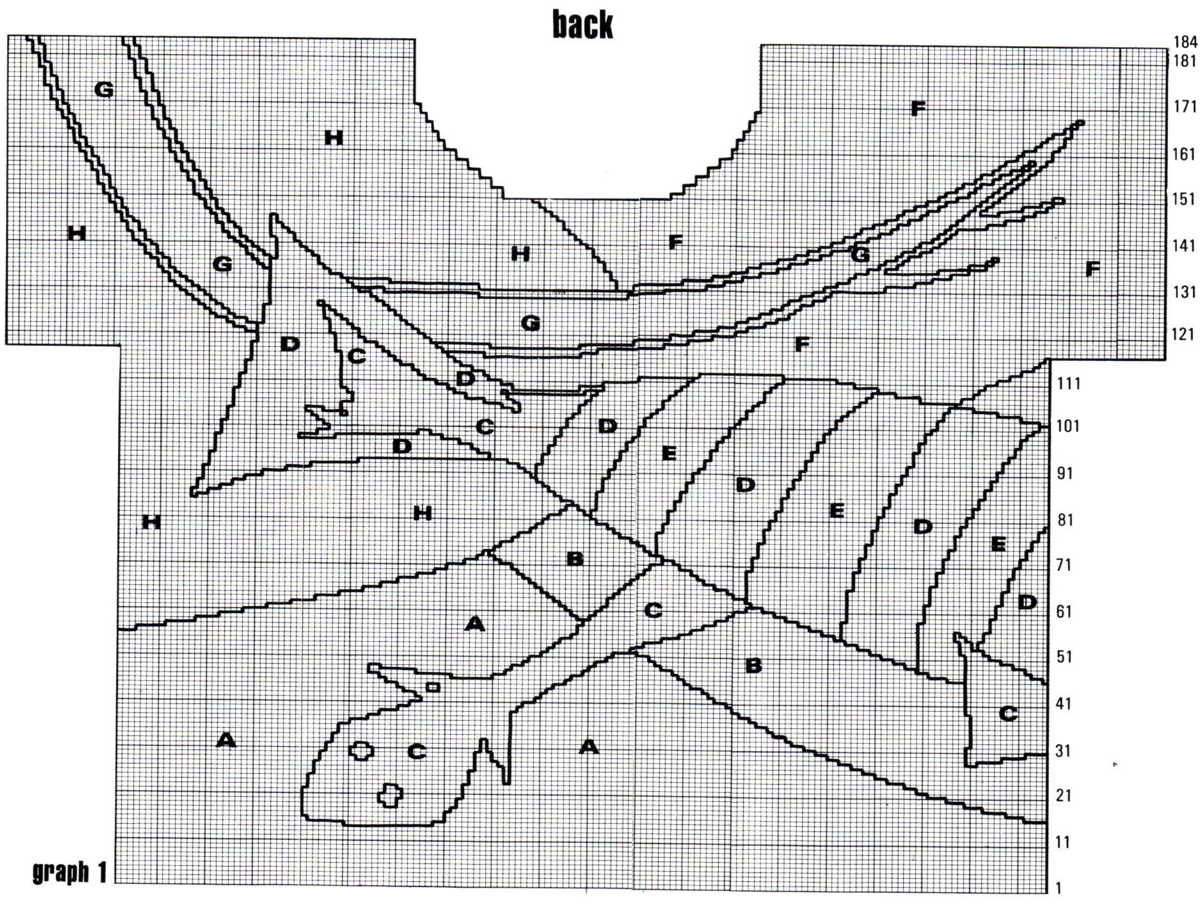

graph 1

front

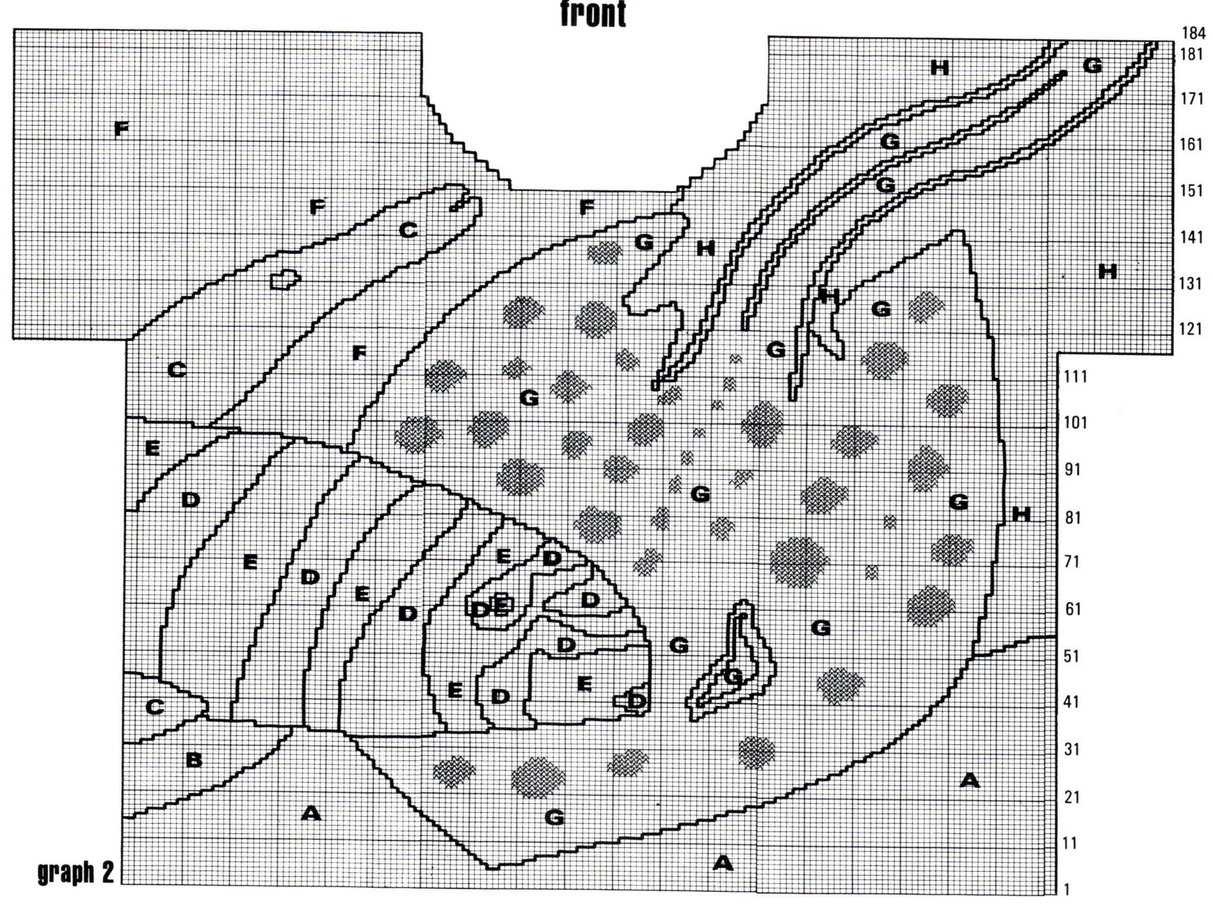

graph 2

MATERIALS

10 colours, see key.
50 g (2 oz) balls of Milford 6 ply Soft Cotton, or equivalent yarn to give stated tension: A 2 balls; B 5 balls; C 1 ball; D 1 ball; E 1 ball; F 3 balls; G 2 balls; H 2 balls; I 1 ball; J 1 ball.
Pair each 4.00 mm (No. 8) and 3.00 mm (No. 11) knitting needles. 7 buttons.

MEASUREMENTS (Garment Measures)

Bust: 111 cm (46½ in)
Length: 63.5 cm (25 in)
Sleeve seam: 50 cm (18 in)

TENSION/GAUGE

22 sts and 26 rows to 10 cm (4 in) over st st in picture knit, using 4.00 mm (No. 8) needles. Change needle size if necessary to obtain the stated tension/gauge.

STITCH DETAILS OF EACH FISH

LARGE FISH IN COLOURS C, F AND G
C section of lower part of face and edges of body at tail end = st st.
F section of tail and main body = double moss st.
G section of face and large spot = double moss st.
G and C section of tail = st st.

THE FISH IN D BACKGROUND AND E SPOTS
D background = st st.
E spots = single moss st.

THE FISH IN I BACKGROUND AND J SPOTS
I background = st st.
J spots = single moss st.

THE CREATURES IN F BACKGROUND AND G SPOTS
F background = st st.
G spots = double moss st.

THE FISH IN C AND G STRIPES
C stripes = garter st.
G stripes = st st.
Eye section in C and G = st st.

NOTE

When working fish in double moss stitch, single moss stitch or garter stitch, always work 1st row of new colour in st st to have a smooth line at change of colour.

SPECIAL ABBREVIATIONS

Double moss stitch (see note)
1st row: (K2, P2) rep over the given number of sts.
2nd row: Knit all knit sts and purl all purl sts.
3rd row: (P2, K2) rep over the given number of sts.

It never fails to amaze me how many different spotty fish jump out at you. The colours under the sea are constantly moving and changing with the light.

4th row: As for 2nd row.
Rep these 4 rows.
Single moss stitch (see note)
1st row: (K1, P1) rep over the given number of sts.
2nd row: Reverse the patt by working K1 over purl st, and P1 over knit st.
Rep these 2 rows.
Garter stitch (g st) (see note)
Knit every row.

BACK

With 3.00 mm (No. 11) needles and A, cast on 135 sts. Work in K1, P1 rib for 7 cm (2¾ in), ending with WS row. Change to 4.00 mm (No. 8) needles and st st. Work from graph 1 until 86 rows have been worked.

SHAPE ARMHOLES
Following graph 1, cast/bind off 2 sts at beg of next 10 rows (115 sts rem). Cont on rem sts until 148 rows of graph have been worked.

SHAPE NECK
Next row: Work 38 sts from graph 1, cast/bind off centre 39 sts, work to end of row. Cont on last 38 sts from graph 1 for left side of neck and dec 1 st at neck edge on next 4 rows (34 sts rem), then work 1 row without dec. Cast/bind off.
Ret to rem 38 sts, rejoin yarn at right neck edge. Following graph 1 for left side of neck, dec 1 st at neck edge on first 4 rows, then work 1 row without dec. Cast/bind off.

LEFT FRONT

With 3.00 mm (No. 11) needles and A, cast on 79 sts. Work in K1, P1 rib for 7 cm (2¾ in), ending with WS row.
Next row: With 4.00 mm (No. 8) needles, work 1st row of graph 1 for left front over 1st 67 sts, leave rem 12 sts on a safety pin for front band.
Beg with 2nd row, work 67 sts, following graph 1 for left front until 86 rows have been worked, ending with WS row.

SHAPE ARMHOLE
Following graph as before, cast/bind off 2 sts at beg of next and every foll alt row 5 times in all. Cont on rem 57 sts from graph until 129 rows have been worked, ending with RS row.

SHAPE NECK
Following graph as before, cast/bind off at beg of next and every foll alt row 5 sts once, 4 sts twice, 3 sts once, 2 sts twice, 1 st 3 times (34 sts rem). Work 8 rows straight from graph. Cast/bind off.

RIGHT FRONT

Work as for left front until rib band measures 2 cm (¾ in) from beg, ending with WS row.
Buttonhole row: Rib 5 sts, cast/bind off centre 3 sts, rib to end.
Next row: Work in rib and cast on 3 sts over centre 3 sts.
Cont in rib until band measures 7 cm (2¾ in) from beg, ending with WS row.
Next row: With 3.00 mm (No. 11) needles, (K1, P1) 6 times and leave these 12 sts on a safety pin for front band, change to 4.00 mm (No. 8) needles, work 1st row of graph 1 for right front over rem 67 sts.
Beg with 2nd row, work from graph 1 for right front until 87 rows have been worked, ending with RS row.

SHAPE ARMHOLE
Following graph as before, cast/bind off 2 sts at beg of next and each alt row 5 times (57 sts rem). Cont on these rem sts following graph until 128 rows have been worked, ending with WS row.

SHAPE NECK
Following graph as before, cast/bind off at beg of next and every foll alt row 5 sts once, 4 sts twice, 3 sts once, 2 sts twice, 1 st 3 times. Cont on rem 34 sts work 9 rows straight from graph. Cast/bind off.

LEFT SLEEVE

With 3.00 mm (No. 11) needles and A, cast on 57 sts. Work in K1, P1 rib for 7 cm (2¾ in), ending with RS row.
Inc row: Rib 6 sts, (inc 1 st in next st, rib 3 sts) rep 11 times, rib 3 sts (69 sts).
Change to 4.00 mm (No. 8) needles and st st.

Following graph 2, inc 1 st each end of 5th row once, then on every foll 6th row 6 times, then every foll 4th row 14 times (111 sts). Work 5 rows straight from graph.

SHAPE TOP

Following graph, cast/bind off 2 sts at beg of next 10 rows (91 sts rem). Work 1 row straight. Cast/bind off.

RIGHT SLEEVE

Work and shape as for left sleeve but following graph 3.

TO MAKE UP

Press lightly on wrong sides. Sew in all ends securely.

LEFT FRONT BAND

With RS facing, slip 12 sts onto 3.00 mm (No. 11) needles, join A at inner edge, inc 1 st in first st (13 sts). Cont in rib as before until band, when slightly stretched fits to neck edge, ending with WS row and dec 1 st at end of last row (12 sts rem). Leave these rem 12 sts on a safety pin. Neatly sew band in position.

BUTTONHOLE BAND (Right Front)

Mark off 7 buttonhole positions on body of jumper starting from 1st one already made, 7th one will be at centre of neck band, 5 others evenly spaced, approximately 27 rows apart.

TO MAKE A BUTTONHOLE

Work 5 sts in rib, on RS row at each marker, cast/bind off centre 3 sts, rib to end. On next row, work in rib and cast on 3 sts over centre 3 sts.

RIGHT FRONT BAND

Work right front band as for left front band with addition of making buttonholes as marked off.

NECKBAND

Sew shoulder seams. With RS facing and A, 3.00 mm (No. 11) needles, (K1, P1) 6 times over right front band, pick up and knit 29 sts on right front neck, 53 sts on back neck, 29 sts on left front neck, (P1, K1) 6 times over left front band (135 sts). Work 3 rows in rib as before, ending with WS row.

Next row: Rib 5 sts, cast/bind off 3 sts, rib to end.

Next row: Work in rib and cast on 3 sts over cast/bind off 3 sts.

Work 4 more rows in rib as before. Cast/bind off ribwise.

TO FINISH

Sew up side seams, taking care to match continuous fish motifs. Sew up sleeve seams. Set sleeves into armholes and sew evenly. Sew on buttons.

right sleeve

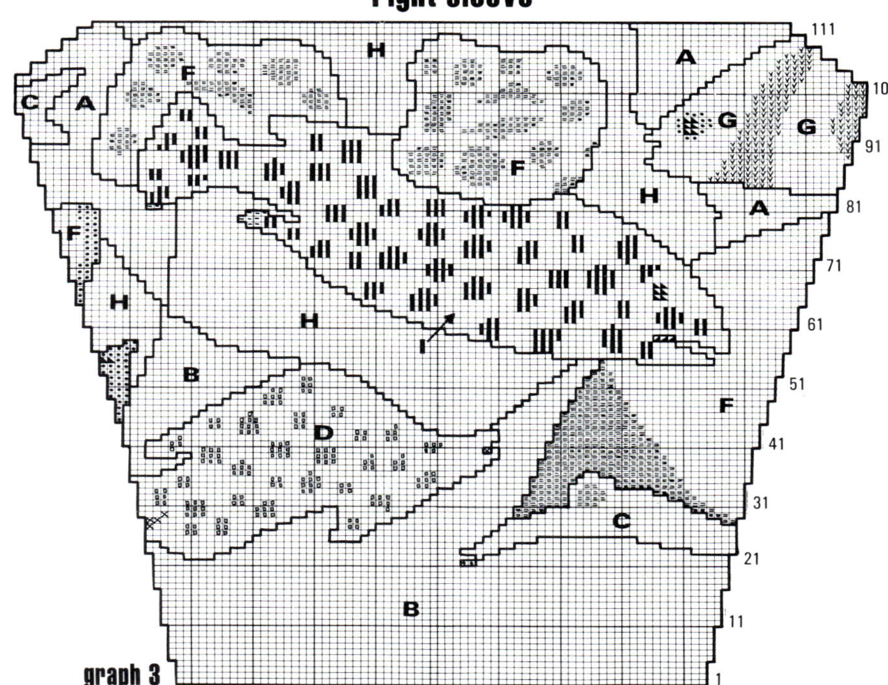

graph 3

left sleeve

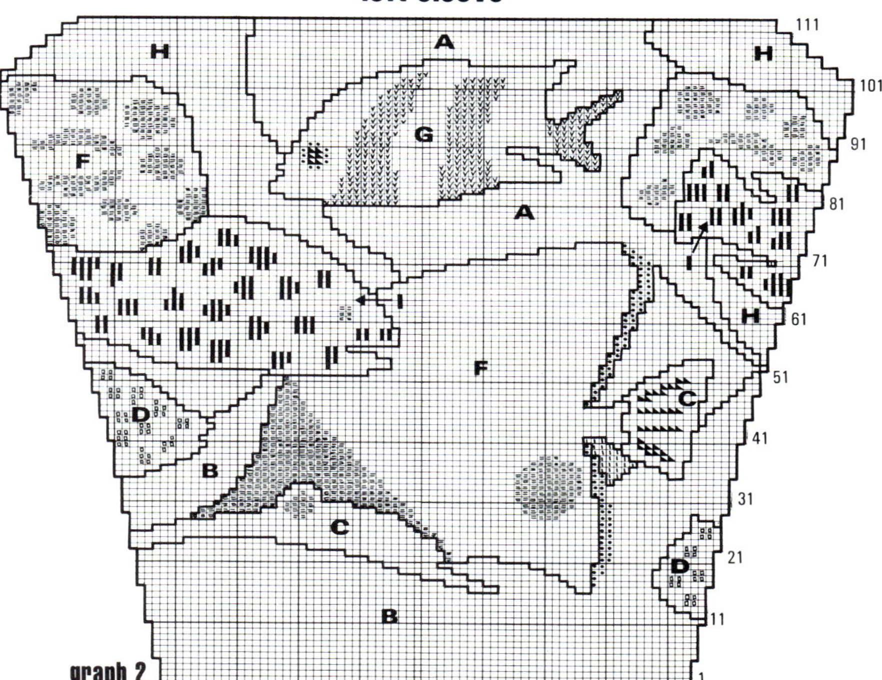

graph 2

KEY
A (Blue)
B (Pink)
C (White)
D (Orange)
E (Emerald)
F (Gold)
G (Black)
H (Lime Green)
I (Red)
J (Purple)
White in garter stitch
Emerald in double moss stitch
Black in double moss stitch
Purple in double moss stitch

front and back

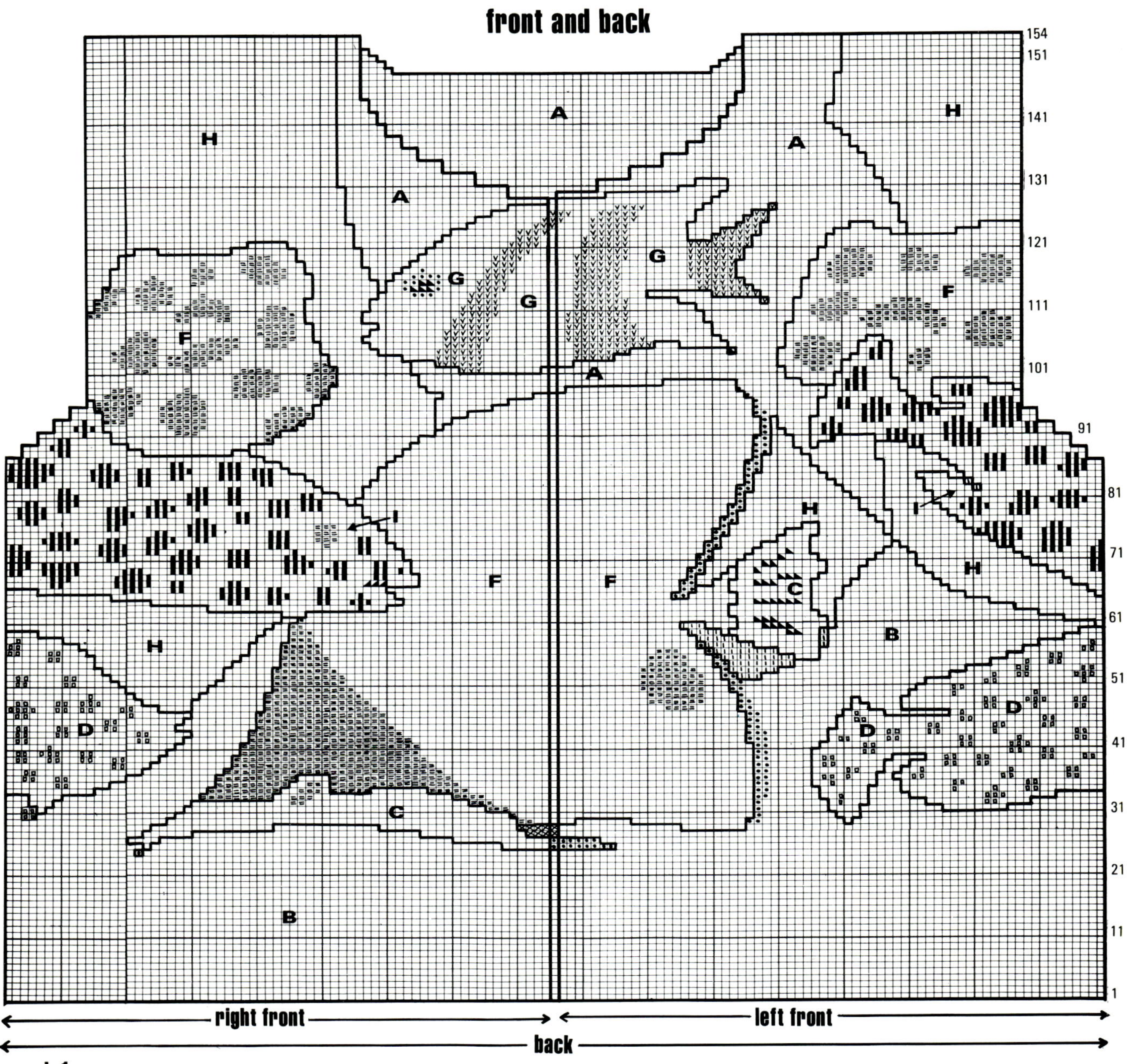

graph 1

MATERIALS
7 colours, see key.
50 g (2 oz) balls of Milford 6 ply Soft Cotton, or equivalent yarn to give stated tension: A 10 balls; B 2 balls; C 1 ball; D 1 ball; E 2 balls; F 2 balls; G 2 balls.
Pair each 4.50 mm (No. 7) and 3.75 mm (No. 9) knitting needles. Set of four 3.00 mm (No. 11) knitting needles.

MEASUREMENTS (Garment Measures)
Bust: 130 cm (51 in)
Length: 100 cm (39½ in)

TENSION/GAUGE
23 sts and 27 rows to 10 cm (4 in) over st st in picture knit, using 4.50 mm (No. 7) needles. Change needle size if necessary to obtain the stated tension/gauge.

BACK
With 3.75 mm (No. 9) needles and A, cast on 146 sts. Work 9 rows in st st. Knit 1 row for hem line. Change to 4.50 mm (No. 7) needles and cont in st st, following graph 1 until 252 rows have been worked.

SHAPE NECK

Next row: Work 64 sts from graph 1, cast/bind off centre 18 sts, work to end of row. Cont on last 64 sts from graph 1, cast/bind off at left neck edge on every alt row 2 sts 4 times, 1 st 3 times (53 sts rem). Work 5 rows straight. Cast/bind off.

Ret to rem 64 sts. Rejoin yarn at right neck edge and cast/bind off at neck edge on next and every foll alt row 2 sts 4 times, 1 st 3 times (53 sts rem). Work 6 rows straight. Cast/bind off.

The beauty of nature is revealed under the sea by the vibrant dance of colours and shapes.

KEY
A (Blue)
B (Red)
C (Green)
D (Orange)
E (Black)
F (Yellow)
G (Pink)

FRONT
Work as for back until hem line has been worked. Change to 4.50 mm (No. 7) needles and cont in st st, following graph 2 until 252 rows have been worked.

SHAPE NECK

Work and finish as for back neck shaping but following graph 2.

TO MAKE UP
Press lightly on wrong sides. Sew in all ends securely. Sew shoulder seams, then sew up side seams, leaving 20 cm (8 in) from shoulders for armholes.

NECKBAND
With RS facing, set of four 3.00 mm (No. 11) needles and A, pick up and knit 20 sts on left side of front neck, 18 sts on centre front neck, 20 sts on right side of front neck, 20 sts on right side of back neck, 18 sts on centre back neck, 20 sts on left side of back neck (116 sts). * Knit 6 rnds, then purl 1 rnd, then knit 6 rnds. Cast/bind off loosely. Fold band in half to inside and stitch down in place.

ARMHOLE BANDS
Both the same. With RS facing, set of four 3.00 mm (No. 11) needles and A, pick up and knit 46 sts on each of back and front piece (92 sts), then work and finish as for neckband from *.

front

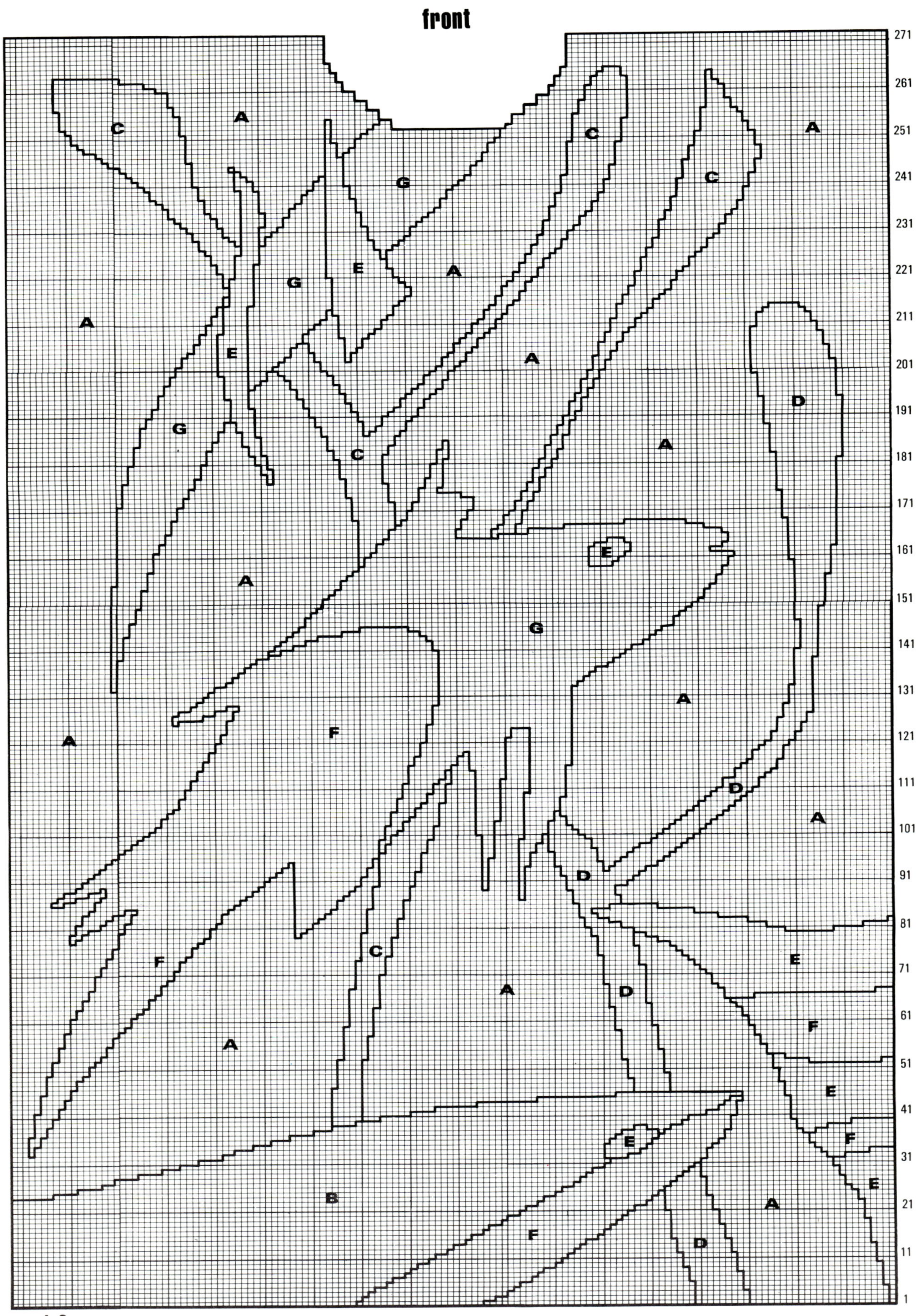

graph 2

back

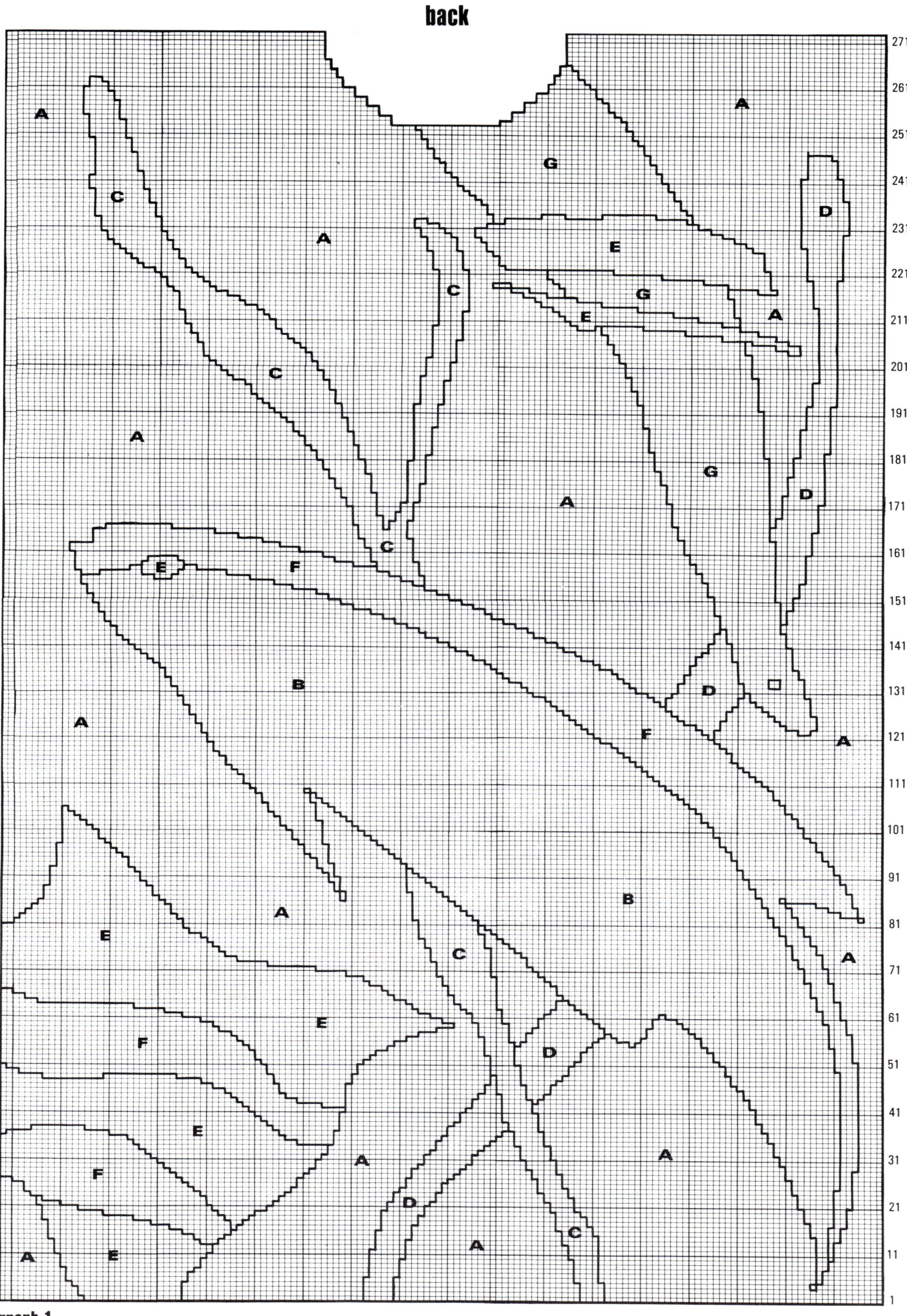
A
C
G
A
D
E
C
A
G
E
A
C
A
D
G
A
C
E
F
B
D
A
F
A
B
C
A
E
E
D
F
E
A
C
A
F
D
A
E
C
A
271
261
251
241
231
221
211
201
191
181
171
161
151
141
131
121
111
101
91
81
71
61
51
41
31
21
11
1

graph 1

MATERIALS
11 colours, see key.
50 g (2 oz) balls of Milford 4 ply Soft Cotton, or equivalent yarn to give stated tension: A 3 balls; B 1 ball; C 1 ball; D 1 ball; E 2 balls; F 1 ball; G 2 balls; H 1 ball; I 2 balls; J 2 balls; K 1 ball.
Pair each 3.25 mm (No. 10) and 2.75 mm (No. 12) knitting needles. Set of four 2.75 mm (No. 12) knitting needles.

MEASUREMENTS (Garment Measures)
Bust: 119 cm (47 in)
Length: 94 cm (37 in)

TENSION/GAUGE
28 sts and 36 rows to 10 cm (4 in) over st st in picture knit, using 3.25 mm (No. 10) needles. Change needle size if necessary to obtain the stated tension/gauge.

BACK
With 2.75 mm (No. 12) needles and A, cast on 171 sts loosely. Work in st st for 3 cm (1¼ in) ending on a knit row. Knit 1 row for hem line. Change to 3.25 mm (No. 10) needles and cont in st st, working from graph until 324 rows have been worked.

SHAPE NECK

Next row: Work 64 sts from graph, cast/bind off centre 43 sts, work from graph to end of row.
Cont on last 64 sts and working from graph, cast/bind off at left neck edge on every alt row 2 sts 4 times (56 sts rem). Work 1 row straight from graph. Cast/bind off.
Ret to rem 64 sts. Rejoin yarn at right neck edge and cast/bind off at neck edge on next and every foll alt row 4 times in all. Work 2 rows straight from graph. Cast/bind off.

The Great Barrier Reef is unique on our earth. Its life is delicately balanced. We are so privileged in Australia to have this tropical sea garden and must protect it against all pollution. It is the greatest national treasure.

FRONT
Work as back until hem line has been worked. Change to 3.25 mm (No. 10) needles and cont in st st. working from graph until 300 rows have been worked.

SHAPE NECK

Next row: Work 71 sts from graph, cast/bind off centre 29 sts, work from graph to end of row.
Cont on last 71 sts and working from graph, cast/bind off at right neck edge on every alt row 2 sts 5 times, 1 st 5 times (56 sts rem). Work 12 rows straight from graph. Cast/bind off.
Ret to rem 71 sts. Rejoin yarn at neck edge and cast/bind off at left neck edge on next and every foll alt row 2 sts 5 times, then 1 st 5 times (56 sts rem). Work 13 rows straight from graph. Cast/bind off.

KEY
- ☐ A (Mid Blue)
- ☒ B (Emerald)
- ⊡ C (Gold)
- ◎ D (Citrus Yellow)
- ▨ E (Red)
- ◣ F (Purple)
- ◢ G (Dark Blue)
- ⊞ H (Orange)
- ⊟ I (Pale Blue)
- ■ J (Hot Pink)
- ☑ K (Lime Green)

TO MAKE UP
Press lightly on wrong sides. Sew in all ends securely. Sew shoulder seams. Sew up side seams, leaving 20 cm (8 in) from shoulder for armholes. Fold hem in half to inside and sew in place.

NECKBAND
With RS facing, set of four 2.75 mm (No. 12) needles and E, beg at left shoulder neck edge, pick up and knit 28 sts on left side of front neck, 29 sts on centre front neck, 28 sts on right side of front neck, 11 sts on right side of back neck, 43 sts on centre back neck, 11 sts on right side of back neck (150 sts). Work in rnds of st st for 3 cm (1¼ in) finishing on wrong side. Purl 1 row on right side, cont in st st for 3 cm (1¼ in). Cast/bind off loosely. Fold band in half to inside, sew in place.

ARMHOLE BANDS
Both the same. With RS facing, set of four 2.75 mm (No. 12) needles and E, pick up and knit 58 sts on each of back and front piece (116 sts). Work in rnds of st st for 3 cm (1¼ in) finishing on wrong side. Purl 1 row on right side, continue in st st for 3 cm (1¼ in). Cast/bind off. Fold band in half to inside and sew in place.

front and back

ACKNOWLEDGEMENTS

The author would like to thank the following people for their invaluable help throughout the production of the book: The yarn companies who so generously provided the wools and cottons — Coats Paton, Georges Picaud, Milford, Robin, Villawool and especially to George Lucas at Cleckheaton. Thanks to the best band of knitters in Australia — Anne, Gloria, Gwen, Helen, Joan, Karen, Kay and Ruth. To Fusako Burton, the pattern writer, for her precise work, Christine Stanton and to Katherine Jarvis and Sue Morton for drawing the graphs.
Thanks also to the two beautiful models, Anna and Kate, to Smilka for her natural styling and hair and make-up and Susie Agoston-O'Connor for her superb design.
Special thanks to my publisher, Kirsty Melville and my editor, Elenie Poulos.

INDEX

Aphrodite jumper 14, 56
Banksia jumper 26, 77
Barramundi jumper 27, 71
Barrier reef jumper 35, 86
Barrier reef skirt 34, 87
Barrier reef top 34, 87
Didgeridoo dolman 28, 80
Dolphins tabard 36, 89
Dolphins top 38, 92
Doves and dolphins jumper 12, 53
Floral oz jumper 19, 62
Football fish tabard 32, 84
Gumleaf jumper 30, 82
I love dolphins jumper 24, 74
Koompartoo jacket 10, 50
Koompartoo vest 10, 48
Pax joy cardigan 21, 64
Pax joy jumper 22, 66
Pax joy leg-ins 21, 67
Pax joy poncho 21, 67
Pax joy skirt 22, 66
Pax scarf 20, 69
Pax socks 20, 68
Pax vest 20, 68
Spotty fish cardigan 41, 96
Stingray top 39, 94
Tropical sea garden dress 42, 102
Ultimate oz jumper 16, 58
Under the sea dress 40, 99
Waratah and blackboy jumper 18, 60